The Sex Addiction Workbook

Information, Assessments, and Tools for Managing Life with a Behavioral Addiction

Ester R.A. Leutenberg and John J. Liptak, EdD

Whole Person Associates

101 West 2nd Street, Suite 203
Duluth, MN 55802-5004

800-247-6789

Books@WholePerson.com
WholePerson.com

The Sex Addiction Workbook

Editorial Director: Jack Kosmach
Art Director: Mathew Pawlak
Cover Design: Adam Sippola
Editor: Peg Johnson

Library of Congress Control Number: 2020947288
ISBN:978-1-57025-364-5

From the co-authors, Ester and John

Our gratitude, thanks, and appreciation

to the following professionals:

— — — — — — — ⚯ ○ ⚯ — — — — — —

Editorial Directors – Jack Kosmach & Peg Johnson

Editor and Life-long Teacher – Eileen Regen, MEd, CIE

Reviewers – Carol Butler Cooper, MS Ed, RN, C and Niki Tilicki, MA Ed

Proof-reader – Jay Leutenberg, CASA

Art Director – Mathew Pawlak

— — — — — — — ⚯ ○ ⚯ — — — — — —

A Special Thank You

to

Whole Person Associates

for their interest in mental health issues.

Free PDF Download Available

To access your free PDF download of the assessment tools
and all of the reproducible activities in this workbook, go to:

https://WholePerson.com/store/TheSexAddictionWorkbook7288.html

Understanding Behavioral Addictions

There are many types of addictions. The addictions that have been talked about most have been substance abuse addictions. However, behavioral addictions can occur that take the same form as a physical dependence on substances. According to the American Addiction Centers (2019):

> ...it is the compulsive nature of the behavior that is often indicative of a behavioral addiction, or process addiction, in an individual. The compulsion to continually engage in an activity or behavior despite the negative impact on the person's ability to remain mentally and/or physically healthy and functional in the home and community defines behavioral addiction. The person may find the behavior rewarding psychologically or get a "high" while engaged in the activity but may later feel guilt, remorse, or even overwhelmed by the consequences of that continued choice. Unfortunately, as is common for all who struggle with addiction, people living with behavioral addictions are unable to stop engaging in the behavior for any length of time without treatment and intervention.
>
> ~American Addiction Centers

People are increasingly experiencing non-substance behavioral addictions and the diminished control over the behaviors they cause. No longer categorized as impulse disorders, behavioral addictions are now being viewed as true addictions much like substance abuse.

Why Are They Called Behavioral Addictions?

**Behavioral addictions constitute any maladaptive pattern of excessive behavior
that manifests in physiological, psychological and cognitive symptoms such as the following:**

- **Continuance:** continuing the behavior despite knowing that this activity is creating or exacerbating physical, psychological and/or interpersonal problems.

- **Intention effects:** Inability to stick to one's routine, as evidenced by exceeding the amount of time devoted to the behavior or consistently going beyond the intended amount.

- **Lack of control:** unsuccessful attempts to reduce the level of the behavior or cease it for a period of time.

- **Reduction in activities:** as a direct result of the behavior, social, familial, occupational, and/or recreational activities occur less often or are stopped.

- **Time:** a great deal of time is spent preparing for, engaging in and recovering from the behavior.

- **Tolerance:** increasing the amount of the behavior in order to feel the desired effect, be it a "buzz" or a sense of accomplishment.

- **Withdrawal:** in the absence of the behavior the person experiences harmful effects such as anxiety, irritability, restlessness, and sleep problems.

The National Institute of Health (2010) states:

Growing evidence suggests that behavioral addictions resemble substance addictions in many domains, including natural history, phenomenology, tolerance, comorbidity, overlapping genetic contribution, neurobiological mechanisms, and response to treatment.

The concept of addiction, for years used to indicate the use of psychotropic substances, is now being applied to describe a heterogeneous group of syndromes known as "behavioral addictions," "no-drug addictions," or "new addictions." Prevalence rates for such conditions are among the highest registered for mental disorders with social, cultural, and economic implications. Individual forms of behavioral addictions are linked by a series of psychopathological features that include: repetitive, persistent, and dysfunctional behaviors, loss of control over behavior in spite of the negative repercussions of the latter, compulsion to satisfy the need to implement the behavior, initial well-being produced by the behavior, craving, onset of tolerance, abstinence, and, ultimately, a progressive, significant impairment of overall individual functioning.

Grant, et al, 2010

Addiction to Sex

The National Council on Sexual Addiction and Compulsivity has defined sexual addiction as "...engaging in persistent and escalating patterns of sexual behavior acted out despite increasing negative consequences to self and others." Therefore, people addicted to sex continue to engage in certain sexual behaviors despite facing potential health risks, financial problems, shattered relationships, and even arrest.

As technology increases in our society, we have seen an increase in the number of individuals engaging in a variety of unusual or illicit sexual practices, such as phone sex, the use of escort services, and computer pornography. Sexual addiction is a progressive intimacy disorder characterized by compulsive sexual thoughts and acts. Like all addictions, its negative impact on the addict and on family members increases as the disorder progresses. Over time, the person usually has to intensify the addictive behavior to achieve the same results. These behaviors can include compulsive masturbation, the extensive use of pornography, routinely accessing phone or computer sex services, as well as illegal activities such as exhibitionism, voyeurism, obscene phone calls, rape or any unwanted sexual actions with another individual.

When sex becomes a problem, it can push people to do things they would not normally do if they were not suffering from an addiction. Behavioral addictions can be challenging to manage. The pages of this workbook are filled with assessments, activities, and journaling exercises that can help your clients or students overcome a sexual addiction and teach them essential skills aimed at helping them repair problems in their lives caused by a preoccupation with sex.

Hypersexual Disorder in the DSM-4

The *Diagnostic and Statistical Manual of Mental Disorders* fourth edition describes sex addiction under the category "Sexual Disorders Not Otherwise Specified" as "distress about a pattern of repeated sexual relationships involving a succession of lovers who are experienced by the individual only as things to be used." According to the manual, sex addiction also involves "compulsive searching for multiple partners, compulsive fixation on an unattainable partner, compulsive masturbation, compulsive love relationships, and compulsive sexuality in a relationship."

The American Psychiatric Association published the fifth edition of its *Diagnostic and Statistical Manual of Mental Disorders*, commonly referred to as the DSM-5. Prior to publication, the APA carefully considered hypersexual disorder (aka, sexual addiction) for inclusion as an official diagnosis. Noted psychiatrist and Harvard Medical School instructor Dr. Martin Kafka prepared the proposed diagnosis for examination by the APA. In doing so, Dr. Kafka reviewed the entire body of sex addiction-focused scientific research and literature, both epidemiological and clinical, and concluded:

> The data reviewed from these varying theoretical perspectives is compatible with the formulation that hypersexual disorder is a sexual desire disorder characterized by an increased frequency and intensity of sexually motivated fantasies, arousal, urges, and enacted behavior in association with an impulsivity component—a maladaptive behavioral response with adverse consequences. Hypersexual disorder can be associated with vulnerability to dysphoric affects and the use of sexual behavior in response to dysphoric affects and/or life stressors associated with such affects.... Hypersexual disorder is associated with increased time engaging in sexual fantasies and behaviors (sexual preoccupation/sexual obsession) and a significant degree of volitional impairment or "loss of control" characterized as disinhibition, impulsivity, compulsivity, or behavioral addiction. Hypersexual disorder can be accompanied by both clinically significant personal distress and social and medical morbidity.

Characteristics of a Healthy Sex Drive

Sexual health includes emotional, psychological, physical, intellectual, and spiritual dimensions. There's no amount of sex that's considered "normal" for everyone. How often you have sex depends on a lot of things, like whether you have a partner, what else is going on in your life, and how strong your desire to have sex (your sex drive) is. People have different sex drives which can change based on things like stress, medications you take, and other physical, emotional, and lifestyle factors. Some people want to have sex every day or more than once a day, and some people hardly ever want to have sex.

A person with a healthy sex drive displays the following characteristics and is able to:

- Accept refusals of sex without expressing hostility or feeling insulted.
- Allow themselves to experience pleasurable sensual and sexual feelings within reason.
- Avoid exploitative relationships with others.
- Be aware of the impact of negative sexual experiences such as personal sexual addiction, sexual abuse, and negative cultural messages pertaining to their sexual development.
- Be comfortable with their sexual identity and orientation.
- Be sensitive to non-verbal cues of their partner's boundaries and limits.
- Communicate and negotiate sexual limits with their partner.
- Communicate respectfully their desires to have sex or not to have sex.
- Communicate with partners their intentions for the relationship *(ex: only dating, want marriage.)*
- Develop friendships that are not sexual in nature.
- Enjoy sexual feelings without necessarily acting upon them.
- Express feelings of desire in ways that do not focus on the genitals *(ex: holding, caressing, kissing.)*
- Feel joy in sexual experiences of their choosing.
- Listen to and respect the boundaries and limits of their partner.
- Realize that, by working through sexual-addiction issues, individuals may heal psychological and emotional wounding from past experiences and damaging beliefs.
- Remain sensually aware and conscious in their bodies.
- Take responsibility for their own bodies and their own orgasms.
- Talk about sexual activity before it occurs, including limits, contraceptive, and condom use.
- Touch their bodies without feeling shame or disgust.
- Understand the capacity to nurture healthy sexual behavior in themselves and others.

This is not an exhaustive list of the characteristics of people with a healthy sex drive. On the next page is a list of the characteristics of people experiencing a sex addiction.

Characteristics of Sex Addiction

For some people, sex addiction can be highly dangerous and result in considerable difficulties with relationships and with the law. Like drug or alcohol dependence, it has the potential to negatively impact people's physical and mental health, personal relationships, quality of life, and safety. As the intensity of a person's preoccupation with sex and sexual behaviors increase, the person is at greater risk of becoming addicted to sex.

A person with a sex addiction displays the following characteristics and may demonstrate some or all of these behaviors:

- Detach when the sexual activity does not emotionally satisfy the individual.

- Engage in frequent attempts to stop the behavior and relapse during times of tension or distress.

- Engage in sexual behaviors for longer than intended, and to a greater extent.

- Experience a sense of shame, guilt, or self-loathing about one's sexual behavior, yet unable to stop.

- Feel irritable when unable to engage in the desired behavior.

- Feel the need to intensify sexual behavior or risk-taking activities in order to achieve the same high.

- Go through a pattern of recurrent failure to resist impulses to engage in extreme acts of lewd sex.

- Have chronic, obsessive sexual thoughts and fantasies.

- Ignore personal obligations or social activities to spend more time indulging in sexual fantasies.

- Lack the ability to set limits or boundaries on sexual urges.

- Lie to cover sexual behaviors.

- Put self or others in danger due to sexual behavior.

- Obsess with attracting others, being in love, and starting new romances.

- Spend an inordinate amount of time pursuing or engaging in sex.

- Undergo sexual rage in which the individual becomes distressed, anxious, restless, and possibly violent if unable to engage in the addiction.

- Use impersonal sources of sexual fulfillment that do not require emotional engagement, such as pornography, prostitution, and cybersex.

- Wind up with negative consequences because of sexual behavior, such as loss of a job, the breakup of a relationship, financial difficulties, or legal problems.

- Yield to compulsive relations with multiple partners, including strangers.

People with a mild sex addiction may exhibit between four and five of these behaviors, while those with a moderately severe sexual addiction may exhibit six to seven. People who suffer from a severe sex addiction will usually exhibit almost all of the behaviors.

Negative Consequences

Left untreated, sex addiction can spiral out of control and lead to extremely negative consequences, causing chaos for the person who has an addiction and his or her family members.

An addiction to sex can also lead to other complications:
- Family issues, relationship problems, and breakups.
- Sexually transmitted illnesses (STIs).
- Financial issues.
- Legal consequences (from illegal sex acts/behaviors or exhibitionism).

Sexual Activities

Sexual activity is a perfectly normal and healthy behavior. However, there is a point when sexual desire can go from being healthy to out of control. Usually, the difference between enjoying sex and being addicted to sex is that a healthy sexual drive can be controlled, but for people who are addicted to sex, the inability or lack of opportunity to engage in sexual acts can be devastating.

Activities associated with sexual addiction:
- Compulsive masturbation.
- Constantly frequenting strip clubs.
- Cybersex.
- Engagement in telephone sex.
- Excessive sexual behavior with consenting adults.
- Exhibitionism.
- Paying prostitutes or practicing prostitution.
- Multiple affairs at one time, sexual-only partners, and one-night stands.
- Pornography.
- Practicing unsafe sex.
- Voyeurism.

People who are addicted to sex tend to continue their behavior despite negative consequences. The sex-related behavior addiction can cause people to do things they wouldn't normally do. Similar to a person addicted to drugs whose life centers on substances, the person addicted to sex finds that life centers on the types of compulsive sexual behaviors noted above. A sex addiction can compromise work, family, relationships, and personal lives.

Withdrawal

Sex addiction signs include withdrawal symptoms when one goes without compulsive sexual behaviors. Like any other addiction withdrawal may include such symptoms such as these:

- Anxiety
- Grumpiness
- Headaches
- Depression
- Restlessness
- Sleep issues
- Cravings
- Agitation
- Irritability

Although the mental and emotional withdrawal symptoms may be intense,
they are a necessary aspect of the recovery process.
Withdrawal is different for every person, however, most people
will exhibit some of the symptoms identified above.

Using This Workbook

The purpose of *The Sex Addiction Workbook* is to provide helping professionals with cognitive and behavioral assessments, tools, and exercises that can be utilized to treat the root psychological causes of a sex addiction. It is designed to help people identify and change negative, unhealthy thoughts and behaviors that may have led to sex addiction. The activities contained in this workbook can help participants identify the triggers that can lead to a preoccupation with sex and teach them ways to manage and overcome those triggers.

The Sex Addiction Workbook will help participants to:

- Recognize that they are experiencing an addiction problem.
- Reflect and become aware of the behaviors that were part of and arose from the addiction.
- Build self-esteem in positive capabilities outside of sexual behavior.
- Understand the triggers for preoccupation with sex.
- Develop greater self-acceptance and the ability to change ineffective behaviors.
- Understand recurring patterns that indicate a sex disorder.
- Learn ways to live a new life without a preoccupation with sex.

The Sex Addiction Workbook is a practical tool for teachers, counselors, and helping professionals in their work with people suffering with behavioral addictions. Depending on the role of the person using this workbook and the specific group's or individual's needs, the modules can be used either individually or as part of an integrated curriculum. The facilitator may choose to administer one activity to a group or administer some of the assessments over one or more days as a workshop.

Confidentiality When Completing Activity Handouts

Participants will see the words "NAME CODES" on some of the activities in the modules. Instruct participants that when writing or speaking about anyone, they should use name codes to preserve privacy and anonymity. These codes will allow participants to explore their feelings without hurting anyone's feelings or fearing gossip, harm, or retribution. For example, a friend named Jack who **W**orks **O**ut **D**aily might be assigned a name code of **W.O.D.** for a particular exercise. In order to protect others' identities, they will not use people's actual names or initials, just NAME CODES.

The Five Modules

This workbook contains five separate modules of activity-based handouts that will help participants learn more about themselves and about their addiction to sex and sex-related behaviors. These modules serve as avenues for self-reflection and group experiences revolving around topics of importance in the lives of the participants in the group.

The activities in this workbook are user-friendly and varied to provide a comprehensive way of analyzing, strengthening, and developing characteristics, skills, and attitudes for overcoming an addiction to sex.

The activities in this workbook are completely reproducible and can be photocopied and/or revised for direct participant use.

Module 1: Sex Addiction Behaviors
This module helps participants explore their unhealthy and unsafe sexual behaviors, sexual fantasies that trigger thoughts of sex, alternatives to unhealthy sexual behavior, ways of dealing with sexual triggers, addiction beliefs, and ways of dealing with emotional pain other than engaging in sex.

Module 2: Social Aspects of a Sex Addiction
This module helps participants explore how their social activities affect their sexual urges, guilt, and shame as an after-effect of unhealthy sexual activities, and peer and social rejection. Participants will identify ways to nurture healthy relationships, methods to deal with feelings of loneliness, and steps to building the amount of physical intimacy in their lives.

Module 3: Escaping Emotional Pain
This module helps participants examine how they may be using unhealthy sexual behaviors to escape from emotional pain in their lives, explore their emotions, understand ways of expressing emotions, deal with shame, and break secrecy about their sexual addiction.

Module 4: Loss of Control
This module helps participants observe the times they are no longer able to control their sexual compulsions, how impulses arise, how they can deal effectively with sexual impulses, be alert to early warning signs of a sexual impulse, and use mindfulness to control sexual impulses.

Module 5: A Hopeful Future
This module helps participants discover ways to promote a healthy and productive future, learn accountability, be more grateful, discover a life purpose, promote positive thinking, overcome feelings of denial, start to determine the type of future they want, explore proud moments, and develop a healthy sex plan.

Different Types of Activity Handouts Included in this Workbook

*Some of the various types of materials
included in this reproducible workbook:*

- **Action Plans** that assist participants in meeting the goals and objectives of treatment.

- **Assessments** that allow participants to explore their behavior.

- **Case Studies** that allow participants the opportunity to apply their thoughts to actual cases.

- **Drawing and Doodling** that unleash the power of the right side of the brain.

- **Educational Pages** that provide insights and tips related to the topic.

- **Group Activities** to encourage collaboration among participants and group brainstorming.

- **Journaling Activities** that can help participants clarify their thoughts and feelings, thus gaining helpful self-knowledge.

- **Positive Affirmations** that allow participants to create formidable affirmations that to be posted and repeated to oneself when impulses begin.

- **Quotation Pages** that allow participants to reflect on many powerful quotes to see how they apply to their own life.

- **Rewards Pages** so that participants remember to reward themselves as they progress toward their goals.

- **Tables** that require participants to reflect on their lives in the past, understand themselves in the present, and react more effectively in the future.

- **And Many More.**

Table of Contents

© 2021 WHOLE PERSON ASSOCIATES, 101 WEST 2ND STREET, SUITE 203, DULUTH MN 55802 • 800-247-6789 • WHOLEPERSON.COM

Table of Contents

(Continued on page xvi)

Table of Contents

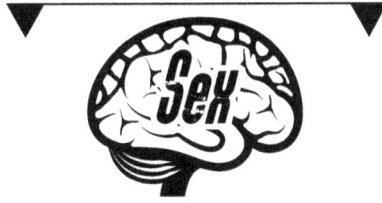

Sex Addiction

Name _____

Date _____

Sex Addiction Behaviors Assessment
Introduction and Directions

People who are addicted to sex engage in sex or think about sex through fantasies and urges more than a normal amount of the time. These individuals may engage in behaviors such as using porn, compulsive masturbation, sex for money, and multiple partners. As a result of these sexual behaviors, these people usually feel distress in all areas of life.

The Sex Addiction Behaviors Assessment is designed to help you explore different types of sexual behaviors in which you may be involved. Read each of the statements and decide if the statement is descriptive of your own sexual behavior.

For each of the items, place a check mark in front of the items that best describe you.

This is not a comprehensive list, but some of the sexual behaviors that one may be excessively engaged in can lead to a sex addiction.

In the following example, the person completing the assessment checked one of three sexual behaviors in which they are engaged excessively:

I am or have been engaging in...

☐ *Actions of obscene, indecent, or unlawful sexual behavior.*

☐ *Acts in which I cannot resist my sexual impulses.*

✓ *Compulsive masturbation.*

Be honest. No one needs to see this if you do not wish to share it.

(Turn to the next page and begin.)

Sex Addiction Behaviors Assessment

I am or have been engaging in...

☐ Actions of obscene, indecent, or unlawful sexual behavior.

☐ Acts in which I cannot resist my sexual impulses.

☐ Affairs with married people.

☐ Compulsive masturbation.

☐ Compulsive viewing of pornography.

☐ Cybersex.

☐ Exhibitionism in which I expose my private parts in public.

☐ Frequent visits to prostitutes.

☐ Habitual visits to strip clubs.

☐ Married and having ongoing affairs with one or more person at the same time.

☐ One-night stands.

☐ Sadistic behavior by inflicting humiliation, bondage, or suffering on others.

☐ Sex in places most people would not normally choose.

☐ Sex to feel wanted, loved, young, attractive, needed.

☐ Sex with a payment involved.

☐ Sexual behavior with an under-age person.

☐ Rape.

☐ Telephone sex.

☐ Unsafe sexual encounters.

☐ Voyeurism in which I observe sexual activity without permission.

Number of items checked = _____

(Go to Scoring Directions on the next page)

Sex Addiction Behaviors Assessment
Scoring Directions & Profile Interpretations

The assessment you just completed is designed to measure the extent to which you are engaging in various addictive sexual behaviors.

Count the number of items you checked on the Sex Addiction Behaviors Assessment.

Put that total on the line marked TOTAL at the end of the section on the assessment. Transfer your total to this space below:

Number of items check marked = _____

~~~~~~

Assessment Profile Interpretation

By checking one item, you are at risk for developing or having a sex addiction. The more items you checked, the greater the risk you have for experiencing a problem with sex and sexual behavior.

Sex Addiction Behaviors Total _____

This assessment measures the extent of your excessive sexual behavior.

Remember that even one checked item can suggest you are experiencing a sex-related addiction. The HIGHER your score on the Sex Addiction Behaviors Assessment, the greater the extent of your sexual addiction.

5 = Low	8 = Moderate	10 = High

What is your reaction to your score?

_____

_____

_____

_____

_____

Chronic, Obsessive Fantasies

One of the things that fuel excessive sexual behavior in sex addicts is chronic, obsessive fantasies. They are triggered from memories, hypothetical situations, and visual stimulation. These fantasies then trigger an urge for sexual satisfaction.

Think about some of the fantasies that fuel your sexual behavior and describe them below:

My Fantasies (USE NAME CODES)	How Often Do They Occur and What Triggers them?	The Fantasy Leads to What Behavior
Example: In my imagination, I am developing a relationship with HTL in a foreign country.	About 3 times per day, usually when I feel rejected by someone.	I go to a local prostitute and ask her to speak with a foreign accent. She thinks I am weird and she can't do a good accent. It leaves me sad.

What is fantasy to you?

_____

_____

_____

Alternatives to Intense Urges

One solution for dealing with intense sexual urges is to find alternative activities in which to engage. This can allow you to distract your unhealthy thinking, redirect your emotions, and substitute healthy activities for the unhealthy ones.

In the blocks below, under each of the headings, write about, doodle, or draw some of the activities that can be used as alternatives to unhealthy sexual behaviors.

Creative Activities	Athletic/Physical Activities	Social Activities

Which category did you have the easiest time completing? What does that say about your interests?

_____

_____

Pattern Awareness

It is vital to be aware of the destructive behavioral patterns that drive your sexual behavior.

In the spaces below, explore your destructive habitual patterns of sexual behavior.

Who is with you when you feel sexual urges? (Use name codes.)
What are you doing or what is typically happening at that moment in your life?
When do these urges occur? In the evening, midday, or morning? Day off from work?
Where are you when they occur?
How do you deal with them when they occur?
Do you believe you manage those urges in a healthy way or an unhealthy way?
What could you do differently to make it healthier? Explain.

Sex Triggers

It is important to identify the triggers that drive your unhealthy, excessive sex habits. When you are more aware of your triggers, you can take action to avoid risky sexual behaviors. Actions may be going for a walk, playing with your pet, exercising, etc.

In the spaces, identify your triggers, when they occur, and how you could distract yourself.

Common Sex Triggers	When These Triggers Occur	How I Can Distract Myself or Avoid the Triggers
Anger		
Anxiety		
Internet-based encounters		
Pornography		
Prior events		
Social rejection		
Sexy stranger		
Loneliness		
Stress		

Some Other Ways to Distract Yourself

Talk with a trusted friend
Try yoga
Meditate
Draw or sketch
Journal, write a poem, etc.

Listen to your favorite music
Watch a non sex-driven movie
Help someone in need
Read inspirational books
Walk in nature

Dealing with Triggers

As a person addicted to sex, it is important to recognize the people, places, and things that trigger your sexual cravings. Once you have identified your triggers, you need to take action to deal with them when they occur.

Following are some ways that you can deal with your sexual cravings. For each of the items listed, identify how you will take action.

1) Block pornography sites. Avoid sexual online chats. How will you do this?

_____

_____

_____

2) Realize that a trigger for sexual acts is an escape from processing your feelings. Talk with a trusted friend or medical professional in order to better understand your feelings as they occur. With whom will you talk?

_____

_____

_____

3) Seek professional assistance and the support of a group-based resource like Sex Addicts Anonymous. Who or where is a support group in your area?

_____

_____

_____

4) Understand the impact loneliness can have on triggering sexual cravings. Make every attempt to connect with people and develop a comprehensive social network to call on when feeling lonely. With whom can you connect when you are lonely?

_____

_____

_____

5) Remember that there will be up and down periods during any recovery. Have a plan for how you will work through difficult situations. What is your plan?

_____

_____

_____

© 2021 WHOLE PERSON ASSOCIATES, 101 WEST 2ND STREET, SUITE 203, DULUTH MN 55802 • 800-247-6789 • WHOLEPERSON.COM

Addiction Beliefs

Most people who engage in excessive sexual habits tend to have strong beliefs about themselves and their behavior. Some of these beliefs are listed below.

On the line under each of the beliefs listed below, place an X on the continuum of how much you relate to the statement. On the dashed line below each one, write why you rated yourself that way. Be HONEST!

I don't need help.

0 (Not Like Me)   5 (Somewhat Like Me)   10 (Much Like Me)

. . . .

I hate myself.

0 (Not Like Me)   5 (Somewhat Like Me)   10 (Much Like Me)

. . . .

I am ashamed of what I do.

0 (Not Like Me)   5 (Somewhat Like Me)   10 (Much Like Me)

. . . .

My actions don't have negative consequences.

0 (Not Like Me)   5 (Somewhat Like Me)   10 (Much Like Me)

. . . .

I don't care about my life.

0 (Not Like Me)   5 (Somewhat Like Me)   10 (Much Like Me)

. . . .

I can stop whenever I want.

0 (Not Like Me)   5 (Somewhat Like Me)   10 (Much Like Me)

. . . .

I face more stress than most people.

0 (Not Like Me)   5 (Somewhat Like Me)   10 (Much Like Me)

. . . .

The HIGHER (Much Like Me) your score on each of the statements, the more of a sexual problem you have in the specific aspect measured. Areas where you scored lower (Not Like Me) suggest that you are not experiencing many signs of a sexual problem in those aspects.

Remember that any scores other than 0 can be indicative of a sexual addiction problem.

My Emotional Pain

Sex addiction is a compulsive behavior that helps the person who is addicted escape from emotional pain (rejection, trauma from the past, loss of significant others, inability to develop healthy intimate relationships, need to be touched and cared about, etc.) and self-medicate. People addicted to sex medicate with compulsive sexual behavior.

In the circles below, identify the causes of your emotional pain. Next to each circle identify a better way to deal with the pain.

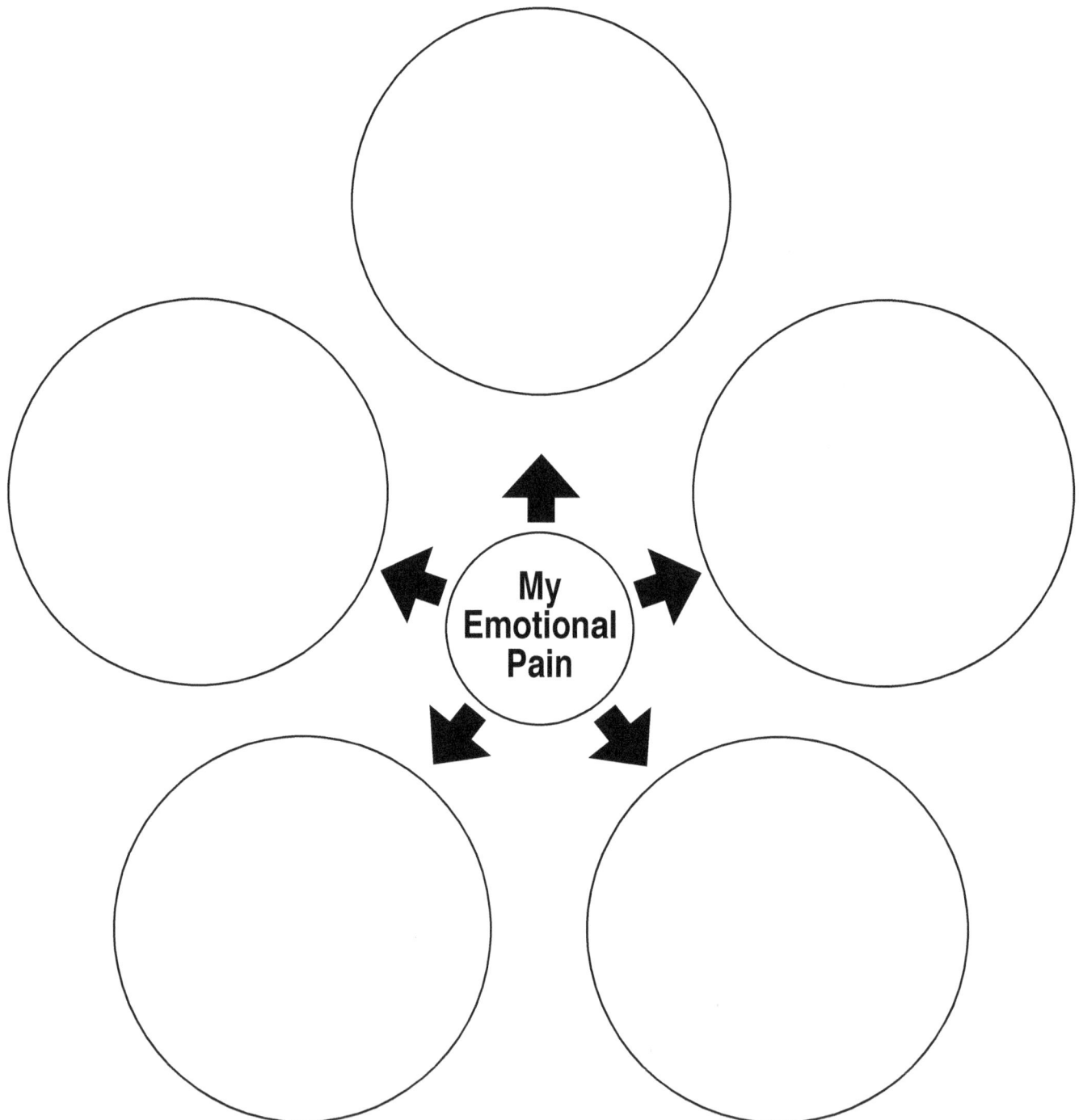

My Emotional Pain

Visual Stimulation

Many people suffering with a sex addiction rely on visual stimulation to trigger a sexual urge and the desire to act out sexually. Some of this visual stimulation might include seeing someone in a social setting or while walking, a photograph in a magazine, mental fantasies, pornographic materials, or images on the internet.

Below, identify your sources of visual stimulation, how you presently react, and how you could overcome this stimulation.

My Sources of Visual Stimulation	How I React	How I Could Overcome the Stimulation
Example: Internet pornography	*Get excited and masturbate.*	*Block pornography.*
Example: Internet pornography	*Get excited and masturbate.*	*Immediately do two minutes of meditation to help clear my mind.*

Additional Ways to Avoid and/or Overcome Visual Stimulation:

- Divert your mind. Call a good friend, read a good non-sexy book, focus on a radio program to take you away from the illusion or to divert you from the stimulation.
- Engage in physical activities such as playing sports, exercising, walking, etc.
- Enjoy social time with friends and family.
- Meditate and practice mindfulness.
- Play computer brain-teasing games.
- Seek counseling.
- Try creative activities such as painting, drawing, or writing.

Endangering Myself and/or Others

Any excessive sexual behaviors in which you are engaging may be putting yourself and others in physical danger by exposure to STIs, HIV/AIDS, unwanted pregnancies, etc. You need to begin thinking about how you may be harming yourself and harming others by your excessive engagement in sexual behaviors.

Below, identify the ways you are exposing yourself to danger by disregarding the potential for physical harm.

Ways I Put Myself in Physical Danger	How I Can Limit the Physical Danger to Myself

Below, identify the ways you are exposing others to danger by disregarding the potential for physical harm.

Ways I Put Myself in Physical Danger	How I Can Limit the Physical Danger to Myself

© 2021 WHOLE PERSON ASSOCIATES, 101 WEST 2ND STREET, SUITE 203, DULUTH MN 55802 • 800-247-6789 • WHOLEPERSON.COM

Characteristics of a Healthy Sex Drive

Sexual health includes emotional, psychological, physical, intellectual, and spiritual dimensions. There's no amount of sex that's considered "normal" for every person. How often you have sex depends on a lot of things, like whether you have a partner, what else is going on in your life, and how strong your sex drive is. People have different sex drives which can change based on things like stress, medications you take, and other physical, emotional, and lifestyle factors. Some people want to have sex every day or more than once a day, and some people hardly ever want to have sex.

Place a check mark in front of the items that apply to you.

I am able to:

☐ Accept refusals of sex without expressing hostility or feeling insulted.

☐ Allow myself to experience pleasurable sensual and sexual feelings within reason.

☐ Avoid exploitative relationships with others.

☐ Be aware of the impact of negative sexual experiences such as personal sexual addiction, sexual abuse, and negative cultural messages pertaining to sexual development.

☐ Be comfortable with my sexual identity and orientation.

☐ Be sensitive to non-verbal cues of my partner's boundaries and limits.

☐ Communicate and negotiate sexual limits with my partner.

☐ Communicate respectfully my desires to have sex or not to have sex.

☐ Communicate with partners my intentions for the relationship *(ex: only dating, want marriage.)*

☐ Develop friendships that are not sexual in nature.

☐ Enjoy sexual feelings without necessarily acting upon them.

☐ Express feelings of desire in ways that do not focus on the genitals *(ex: holding, caressing, kissing.)*

☐ Feel joy in sexual experiences of my choosing.

☐ Listen to and respect the boundaries and limits of my partner.

☐ Realize that, by working through sexual-addiction issues, individuals may heal psychological and emotional wounding from past experiences and damaging beliefs.

☐ Remain sensually aware and conscious in my body.

☐ Take responsibility for my own body and my own orgasms.

☐ Talk about sexual activity before it occurs, including limits, contraceptive and condom use.

☐ Touch my own body without feeling shame or disgust.

☐ Understand the capacity to nurture healthy sexual behavior in myself and others.

The more items you checked, the greater your ability to experience a healthy sex drive.

Characteristics of Sex Addiction

For some people, sex addiction can be highly dangerous and result in considerable difficulties with relationships and with the law. Like drug or alcohol dependence, it has the potential to negatively impact people's physical and mental health, personal relationships, quality of life, and safety. As the intensity of people's preoccupation with sex and sexual behaviors increases, they are at greater risk of becoming addicted to sex.

Place a check mark in front of the items that apply to you.

I often:

☐ Detach so that the sexual activity does not emotionally satisfy.

☐ Engage in frequent attempts to stop the behavior and relapse during times of tension or distress.

☐ Engage in sexual behaviors for longer than intended, and to a greater extent.

☐ Experience a sense of shame, guilt, or self-loathing about my sexual behavior, yet am unable to stop.

☐ Feel irritable when unable to engage in the desired behavior.

☐ Feel the need to intensify sexual behavior or risk-taking activities in order to achieve the same high.

☐ Go through a pattern of recurrent failure to resist impulses to engage in acts of lewd sex.

☐ Have chronic, obsessive sexual thoughts and fantasies.

☐ Ignore personal obligations or social activities to spend more time indulging sexual fantasies.

☐ Lack the ability to set limits or boundaries on sexual urges.

☐ Lie to cover sexual behaviors.

☐ Put self or others in danger due to sexual behavior.

☐ Obsess with attracting others, being in love, and starting new romances.

☐ Spend an inordinate amount of time pursuing or engaging in sex.

☐ Undergo sexual rage in which I become distressed, anxious, restless, and possibly violent if unable to engage in the addiction.

☐ Use impersonal sources of sexual fulfillment that do not require emotional engagement, such as pornography, prostitution, and cybersex.

☐ Wind up with negative consequences because of sexual behavior, such as the loss of a job, the breakup of a relationship, financial difficulties, or legal problems.

☐ Yield to compulsive relations with multiple partners, including strangers.

People with a mild sex addiction may exhibit four or five of these behaviors, while those with a moderately severe sexual addiction may exhibit six or seven. People who suffer from a severe sex addiction will usually exhibit most all of the behaviors.

Interference with Daily Life

Your sexual activities might be interfering with other healthy activities and your obligations.

Below, identify how your sexual activities are interfering with various aspects of your life.

Areas of My Life	How It is Being Affected	How It Will Hurt Me/Others
Example: My Job	*I look at porn on my work computer.*	*I would lose my job if I got caught.*
My Job		
My Family Relationships		
My Friend Relationships		
My Finances		
My Legal Life		
My Hobbies/Recreation		
Other		

When everything seems to be going against you, remember that
the airplane takes off against the wind, not with it.
~ Henry Ford

My Efforts to Stop

You might have already tried to stop your unhealthy sexual activities. Some of these efforts may have been more successful than others.

Effort 1

Effort 2

Effort 3

Which efforts were successful and why? _____

Which efforts were NOT successful and why? _____

What will be different this time? _____

Sex Addiction Symptoms Page 1

Below are some of the symptoms that are typical of people who have a sex addiction. *Place a check mark in front each one of the symptoms that apply to you and then write how they affect your life.*

☐ Failure to resist sexual impulses in order to engage in compulsive sexual behaviors.

_____
_____
_____

☐ Engage in sexual behaviors to a greater extent, or over a longer period of time than intended.

_____
_____
_____

☐ Persistent desire or unsuccessful efforts to stop or control sexual behaviors.

_____
_____
_____

☐ Engage in sexual behavior when expected to fulfill occupational, academic, domestic, or social obligations.

_____
_____
_____

☐ Continuation of sexual behavior despite recurrent social, psychological, relationship, or marital problems, caused by the behavior.

_____
_____
_____

☐ Give up or limit social, occupational, or recreational activities due to sexual behavior.

_____
_____
_____

☐ Distress, anxiety, restlessness, or irritability if unable to engage in sexual behavior.

_____
_____
_____

(Continued on the next page)

Sex Addiction Symptoms Page 2

☐ Compulsive sexual relations with multiple partners, including strangers.

_____

_____

_____

☐ Preoccupation with having sex, even when it interferes with daily life.

_____

_____

_____

☐ Inability to stop or control sexual behaviors.

_____

_____

_____

☐ Putting oneself or others in danger due to sexual behavior.

_____

_____

_____

☐ Feeling remorse or guilt after engaging in sexual behavior.

_____

_____

_____

☐ Experiencing legal and financial consequences from sexual behavior.

_____

_____

_____

You had the choice of checking off 13 different items on the two Symptoms Pages. The more items you checked, the deeper your sexual addiction problem is.
- If you checked off 0 items, your sexual addiction problem is limited.
- If you checked off 1-4 items, you have a slight sexual addiction problem.
- If you checked off 5-9 items, you have a moderate sexual addiction problem.
- If you checked off 10-13 items, you have a severe sexual addiction problem.

Quotes about Sexual Activities

On the lines that follow each of the quotes, describe what they mean
to you and how they apply to YOUR life.

In so far as one denies what is, one is possessed by what is not, the compulsions,
the fantasies, the terrors that flock to fill the void.
~ Ursula K. Le Guin

_____

_____

_____

All fixed set patterns are incapable of adaptability or pliability.
The truth is outside of all fixed patterns.
~ Bruce Lee

_____

_____

_____

Our inner beliefs trigger failure before it happens. They sabotage lasting change by
canceling its possibility. We employ these beliefs as articles of faith to justify our
inaction and then wish away the result. I call them belief triggers.
~ Marshall Goldsmith

_____

_____

_____

I feared vulnerability more than my actual emotional pain itself!
~ Karen Salmansohn

_____

_____

_____

Which quote especially speaks to you and your sex addiction? Why?

_____

_____

_____

_____

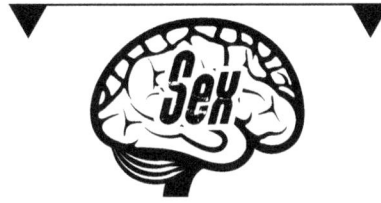

Social Aspects

Name _____

Date _____

Social Aspects
Introduction and Directions

A sexual addiction can develop due to factors in an individual's life. However, social life is often the strongest factor tied to one's excessive sexual behaviors and the ultimate development of a sex disorder.

The following assessment contains 18 statements related to the social aspects of your addiction to sex. This assessment can help you to gauge your level of awareness of the effect of engagement in excessive, unhealthy sexual activity in your life.

Read each of the statements and decide whether or not the statement describes you.

If the statement describes you, circle the number in the YES column next to that item.
If the statement does not describe you, circle the number in the NO column next to that item.

In the following example, the circled 2 indicates that the person completing this assessment believes that the statement describes him or her:

	YES	NO

When it comes to social relationships, I:

Feel lonely. . . . . (2) 1

This is not a test. Since there are no right or wrong answers, do not spend too much time thinking about your answers. Be sure to respond to every statement.

(Turn to the next page and begin.)

Social Aspects of a Sex Addiction Assessment

Name _____ Date _____

	YES	NO

When it comes to social relationships, I:

	YES	NO
Feel lonely.	2	1
Feel unworthy of the love of others.	2	1
Don't feel good about myself.	2	1
Feel guilt and shame.	2	1
Fear being rejected.	2	1
Worry that others will find out who I am.	2	1

Relationships – TOTAL = _____

In my healthy, intimate relationships, I:

	YES	NO
Don't offer appropriate communication during sex.	2	1
Am controlling during sexual activity.	2	1
Have frequent mood swings before or after sex.	2	1
Am demanding about sex regarding time and place.	2	1
Lack intimacy before, during, and/or after sex.	2	1
Offer little or no genuine intimacy in the relationship.	2	1

Intimacy – TOTAL = _____

I have harmed my social relationships by:

	YES	NO
Hiding and looking at pornographic material.	2	1
Encouraging others to engage in excessive sexual activity.	2	1
Always having a good reason to look at pornography.	2	1
Frequently renting or streaming pornographic material.	2	1
Becoming angry if someone is concerned about my sex addiction.	2	1
Hiding my medical problems due to sexual activity.	2	1

Harm – TOTAL = _____

*Go to the next page for scoring assessment
results, profile interpretation, and individual descriptions*

© 2021 WHOLE PERSON ASSOCIATES, 101 WEST 2ND STREET, SUITE 203, DULUTH MN 55802 • 800-247-6789 • WHOLEPERSON.COM

Social Aspects of a Sex Addiction Assessment

Scoring Directions & Profile Interpretations

The assessment you just completed is designed to measure the ways your sex addiction has affected your social relationships.

In each of the sections on the previous page, count the scores you circled. Put that number on the line marked TOTAL at the end of each section. Transfer your total to the space below, and place an X on the line representing your score:

Relationships _____ (Your willingness and ability to engage in relationships with other people.)

| 6 = Low | 9 = Moderate | 12 = High |

Intimacy _____ (Your level of intimacy with spouses and partners in close relationships.)

| 6 = Low | 9 = Moderate | 12 = High |

Harm _____ (The harm to your personal relationships because of your sexual habits.)

| 6 = Low | 9 = Moderate | 12 = High |

Assessment Profile Interpretation

Individual Scale Scores	Results	Indications
6 to 7 in any single area	Low	Low scores indicate that you have a limited number of social aspects that are affecting your personal relationships.
8 to 10 in any single area	Moderate	Moderate scores indicate that have some social aspects that are definitely affecting your personal relationships.
11 to 12 in any single area	High	High scores indicate that you have many social aspects that are definitely affecting your personal relationships.

Remember that even one circled item on a scale can suggest you are experiencing a sex-related addiction.

The HIGHER your score on the Social Aspects Assessment, the greater the effect your sexual addiction is having on your social relationships.

My Unhealthy Episode Story

People addicted to sex are often unable to form and sustain intimate relationships and/or close friendships. This is often due to a lack of self-esteem based on an inability to forgive themselves. It can be difficult to forgive oneself for unhealthy sex habits in the present or in the past.

Respond to the questions below. Use NAMES CODES.

What was your unhealthy sex episode?

_____
_____
_____

Where were you at the time?

_____
_____
_____

What had just happened prior to the episode?

_____
_____
_____

Who was with or around you?

_____
_____
_____

What did you need and from whom?

_____
_____
_____

What were you thinking?

_____
_____
_____

How could you have coped in a better way?

_____
_____
_____

Guilt and Shame

Many people who are addicted to sex experience feelings of guilt and shame after engaging in an unhealthy sexual activity.

Write about the last time you engaged in a sexual behavior as a result of your being addicted to sex.

_____

_____

_____

Now explore the various feelings associated with this event.

I was ashamed that I:

I felt the shame in my:

The shame affected me when I tried to:

I felt guilty because:

My guilt forced me to:

I wish I could express my feelings to:

Maintaining My Addiction

People with a sex-related addiction often resort to telling lies in an attempt to cover up their addiction and its consequences. They lie to others to maintain the cycle of their addiction. They lie to work supervisors, intimate partners, family members, friends, and people in their communities in order to hide their secret life.

Think about some of the ways that you have told lies to cover up your sexual habits. Below, identify the people to whom you lie, how you lie, and the consequences of your behavior. Be honest! No one else needs to see this if you choose. It can be only for you.

Person To Whom I Lie and Our Relationship USE NAME CODES.	The Reason(s) I Lie	The Excuses I Provide
Example: PLR - Work	I am just too tired to go to work.	I say I am not feeling well to cover up the true reasons for my missing work.

A harmful truth is better than a useful lie.
~ Thomas Mann

© 2021 WHOLE PERSON ASSOCIATES, 101 WEST 2ND STREET, SUITE 203, DULUTH MN 55802 • 800-247-6789 • WHOLEPERSON.COM

Peer Rejection

People addicted to sex often fear that others will find out about their secret life. They are afraid they will face judgment and/or rejection from their peers. This can limit the amount of their participation in a normal social life.

What are some of the social situations you avoid because of your fear of rejection? Put them, and why you fear rejection in this situation, in the spaces below.

Fear of
Rejection

Nurture Healthy Relationships

In most cases, people addicted to sex are unable to foster healthy relationships. They are usually lying to friends about their whereabouts and living two separate lives.

What are some of the healthy relationships that you do not have, but wish you did?

Relationships I Wish I Had USE NAME CODES.	Why We Don't Have The Relationship I Would Like to Have	How I Could Reestablish or Begin Each of the Relationships
Example: My best friend J.L.C.	*He can go to a movie only on Sunday nights. That is one of my nights to get out of the house and have sex.*	*I could go to a movie with him once in a while and give up sex that night, and if it works out okay, go to movies more often with other people.*

A healthy relationship is built on unwavering trust.
~ Beau Mirchoff

I'm Lonely

Many people who are addicted to sex feel alone and lonely, and turn to unhealthy sex acts to compensate for this feeling of loneliness. Soon after, they fear being lonely, and they turn to unhealthy sex again. It's a vicious cycle.

They find it difficult to begin and develop healthy sexual relationships because of their addiction, so they are reluctant to initiate relationships.

In the spaces below, identify some of your fears of being lonely, not accepted, boredom, etc. To the right of the fear, provide more rational thinking to dispute the fear.

My Fears

Example: What if I make friends with someone and that person finds out about my sex habit, and will dump me and I will be lonely again. More rational thinking might be that the person may be able to help me find ways to kick my sex habit!

MY FEAR   **More Rational Thinking**

_____

_____

_____

_____

_____

MY FEAR   **More Rational Thinking**

_____

_____

_____

_____

_____

Intimacy

Most people think of intimacy as it relates to sex and physical lovemaking. However, there are many other types of intimacy you can feel with a partner. The more intimate you can be, the less you will need to rely on unhealthy sexual acts.

In each of the two sections below—Emotional Intimacy and Cognitive Intimacy—place a check mark in front of those that apply to you and an intimate friend or partner, and write a few words to describe the action in your relationship.

EMOTIONAL INTIMACY

☐ I am able to connect on an emotional level with my partner.

_____

☐ I am able to communicate my feelings of love.

_____

☐ I am able to express my feelings when I am angry.

_____

☐ I am able to express my feelings in a comfortable, unguarded way.

_____

☐ My partner constructively receives and responds to the expression of my feelings.

_____

☐ I am emotionally close with my partner.

_____

☐ I am not afraid to express my feelings at any time.

_____

☐ I trust my partner enough to say anything.

_____

COGNITIVE INTIMACY

☐ I can share my most private thoughts with my partner.

_____

☐ I feel like I can trust my partner when I share intimate information.

_____

☐ I often bounce ideas off of my partner for a second opinion.

_____

☐ I am able to communicate my needs and desires to my partner.

_____

☐ I feel comfortable sharing my most intimate needs with my partner.

_____

☐ I am not afraid to tell my partner about my secrets.

_____

☐ I often talk with my partner about our future together.

_____

☐ I feel a deep level of trust with my partner.

_____

After reviewing your check marks above—how would you rate your intimacy level with your partner with Zero (0) being the lowest and ten (10) being the highest? How safe do you feel in asking your partner to also fill out the same activity and then rate it?

My Physical Intimacy

Many people addicted to unhealthy sex believe that they do not have enough sexual satisfaction in a healthy intimate relationship.

On the line under each example of the ability to control sexual urges, place an X on the continuum of how much you relate to the statement. On the dotted line below each one, write why you rated yourself that way.

I have a physically intimate relationship with my partner.

0 (Not Like Me)　　　　　5 (Somewhat Like Me)　　　　　10 (Much Like Me)

. . . .

I often show my significant other affection in public.

0 (Not Like Me)　　　　　5 (Somewhat Like Me)　　　　　10 (Much Like Me)

. . . .

My partner is physically intimate with me.

0 (Not Like Me)　　　　　5 (Somewhat Like Me)　　　　　10 (Much Like Me)

. . . .

I show my deep love for my partner through sexual intimacy.

0 (Not Like Me)　　　　　5 (Somewhat Like Me)　　　　　10 (Much Like Me)

. . . .

My partner satisfies my needs sexually.

0 (Not Like Me)　　　　　5 (Somewhat Like Me)　　　　　10 (Much Like Me)

. . . .

I am aware of and I am able to meet my partner's intimate needs.

0 (Not Like Me)　　　　　5 (Somewhat Like Me)　　　　　10 (Much Like Me)

. . . .

I do not need to seek out unhealthy sexual activities.

0 (Not Like Me)　　　　　5 (Somewhat Like Me)　　　　　10 (Much Like Me)

. . . .

Social Support

Not only does social isolation increase a sex addict's likelihood of seeking unhealthy ways of being sexually gratified, it also leads to a host of other problems like health issues and financial issues.

Describe how you can reach out to supportive people in your life to avoid being isolated.

Potential Person to Support Me and Whom I Could Support (USE NAME CODES)	How This Person Can Support Me	How I Can Support This Person
Example: KAM	*She is very trustworthy and under-standing. I can call and talk to her when I am ready to do something foolish.*	*She has a bad back. I can be more available to her, and let her know that I can help out at any time.*

Get Involved

People who are managing their addiction to sex make it a point to enjoy active participation in educational, cultural, and community activities outside of the classroom, home, workplace and/or volunteer job. These activities can provide respite from sexual urges.

What types of educational, cultural, and community activities do you enjoy?

Activity	Where and When I Do It	Why I Enjoy It

Think about the types of educational, cultural, and community activities you have done before, or have never done before, but might enjoy doing.

Activity	Where I Could Become Involved	Why Haven't I Been doing This Lately?

The Quality of My Human Relationships

I can't stress this enough: The single thing that will guarantee a happy,
fulfilled, and calmer life is the quality of your human relationships,
especially the people you love and who love you back.

~ Joanna Coles

What does the above quote mean to you?

_____

_____

_____

How would you describe the quality of your human relationships?

_____

_____

_____

How do (or can) your human relationships make you happier and more fulfilled?

_____

_____

_____

How do (or can) your human relationships help you to be calmer?

_____

_____

_____

Who are the people you love and who love you back?

_____

_____

_____

How can these same people help you to overcome your addiction to sex?

_____

_____

_____

© 2021 WHOLE PERSON ASSOCIATES, 101 WEST 2ND STREET, SUITE 203, DULUTH MN 55802 • 800-247-6789 • WHOLEPERSON.COM

Sending Emotional Messages

Some people are unable to express themselves to their partner regarding sex. Emotional messages can help one to communicate one's wants and needs to one's intimate partners. Having a healthy open conversation about sex with a partner, can eliminate the need to seek other sexual activities with other people.

Complete the following statements about the emotionally-driven messages you would like to send to your partner. Then ask your partner to do the same.

You hurt my feelings when you_____
_____

I feel unappreciated when you _____
_____

I get scared when you_____
_____

I am thankful that you _____
_____

I like it when you _____
_____

I want you to be more _____
_____

I want you to be less_____
_____

I get excited when you _____
_____

I wish we could_____
_____

I wish we would_____
_____

Better Communication Skills

In order to develop and maintain healthy, intimate relationships, it will help to hone your basic communication skills.

Following are some ways that you can be a better communicator. Place a check mark in front of skills you already use and write about how effective it is.

☐ Be assertive by being open, honest, and direct.

_____

☐ Don't interrupt others when they are speaking—just listen.

_____

☐ Send direct, clear, verbal messages.

_____

☐ Cope without anger in difficult conversations.

_____

☐ Describe your feelings rather than attacking with them.

_____

☐ Pay attention to body language and gestures as well as tone, volume, and pitch of voice.

_____

☐ Ask for what you want and need in a respectful way.

_____

☐ Be careful how many times you say, "Yes, but ... ."

_____

☐ Focus your full attention on the speaker rather than being distracted.

_____

☐ Do not gossip or repeat gossip.

_____

☐ Be aware of your body language. *(Good eye contact, good posture, arms uncrossed, open stature, no fists, sincere smile, etc.)*

_____

☐ Avoid blaming and accusing.

_____

☐ Avoid global labels like stupid, silly, nuts, crazy, and loony.

_____

Now, highlight those skills you will commit yourself to on a regular basis.

Partner Exploration

People who have a difficult time maintaining a healthy intimate relationship, often turn to unhealthy sexual behaviors for satisfaction. The following questions are intended to help you explore (and remember) what you enjoyed about one of your ex-partners.

Respond to the following questions as truthfully as possible and think about how they can help you to be aware of the type of partner who would be a good match for you. Explain what you learned.

Name code of one of my ex-partners whom I truly cared about: __ __ __

The thing I loved best about this person was _____
_____
_____

I wish I would have told this person that _____
_____
_____

The things that made us a great couple were _____
_____
_____

The things that made us a lousy couple were _____
_____
_____

I appreciated the way this partner _____
_____
_____

I don't think I appreciated the following characteristics about this partner, but I do now _____
_____
_____

I appreciated the way my partner handled this situation_____
_____
_____

I was a better person when I was with this partner because_____
_____
_____

I was not a better person when I was with this partner because _____
_____
_____

From this relationship I learned _____
_____
_____

Fair Fighting

Conflict occurs in all relationships, but can occur more often for people who have an addiction. Because they often live a double life filled with secrecy and hiding, their relationships are prone to more conflict.

Think about the last time you and an intimate partner had a conflict as a result of one of your unhealthy sexual behaviors.

Our last argument was about_____

_____

_____

Then, respond to the following questions:

What was your side of the argument?_____

_____

_____

What was your partner's side of the argument?_____

_____

_____

What triggered the argument? _____

_____

_____

What feelings were expressed in this argument? _____

_____

_____

What was the outcome of this argument? _____

_____

_____

What could your partner have done to help you? _____

_____

_____

How could you avoid or handle this type of argument differently in the future? _____

_____

_____

Quotes about Intimate Relationships

On the lines that follow each of the two quotes, describe
what speaks to you and your intimate relationships.

Times may have changed, but there are some things that are always with us –
loneliness is one of them.
~ Laurie Graham

_____

_____

_____

_____

_____

_____

Most fears of rejection rest on the desire for approval from other people.
Don't base your self-esteem on their opinions.
~ Harvey Mackay

_____

_____

_____

_____

_____

_____

Which quote especially speaks to you and your intimate relationships? Why?

_____

_____

_____

_____

_____

_____

_____

_____

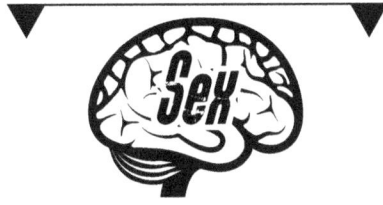

Escaping Emotional Pain

Name _____

Date _____

Escaping Emotional Pain Assessment
Introduction and Directions

The engagement in excessive, unhealthy sex is often an attempt by people to escape some type of emotional pain. Because they may lack the coping skills to deal with their emotional pain, they sometimes resort to sex in order to feel better.

The *Escaping Emotional Pain Assessment* is designed to help you explore whether you are stuck in the cycle of emotional pain leading to sex, thus leading back to emotional pain. The assessment contains statements divided into five categories.

Read each of the statements and decide if it is descriptive of you. In each of the choices listed, circle the number of your response on the line to the right of each statement.

In the following example, the circled 2 indicates the statement is LIKE the person completing the inventory:

	LIKE ME	UNLIKE ME

Related to my sexual addiction...

I have experienced trauma in my past. . . . . (2) 1

This is not a test. Since there are no right or wrong answers, do not spend too much time thinking about your answers. Be sure to respond to every statement.

(Turn to the next page and begin.)

Escaping Emotional Pain Assessment

Name _____ Date _____

	LIKE ME	UNLIKE ME

Related to my sexual addiction...

I have experienced trauma in my past. 2 1

I am experiencing marriage and/or family problems. 2 1

I worry about everything. 2 1

I am under significant stress. 2 1

I feel guilty about my past. 2 1

I. Pain – TOTAL = _____

	LIKE ME	UNLIKE ME

Related to my sexual addiction...

I engage in unhealthy sex to escape from my thoughts. 2 1

I fantasize about sex to avoid emotions. 2 1

I use sex to disconnect from reality. 2 1

I use sex to ease my inner turmoil. 2 1

I believe that sex allows me to manage my stress. 2 1

II. Escape – TOTAL = _____

	LIKE ME	UNLIKE ME

Related to my sexual addiction...

I regularly engage in unhealthy sexual behavior. 2 1

I have specific routines prior to engaging in unhealthy sex. 2 1

I become irritable when I am not engaging in sex. 2 1

Sex is a vital part of my daily life. 2 1

My lifestyle and schedule revolve around my sexual habits. 2 1

III. Action – TOTAL = _____

(Continued on the next page)

Escaping Emotional Pain Assessment (page 2)

	LIKE ME	UNLIKE ME

Related to my sexual addiction...

Engaging in sex is more significant to me than the consequences. 2 1

I engage in risky sexual behaviors. 2 1

I feel as if my risky sexual behaviors are getting worse. 2 1

I am putting myself and others in danger. 2 1

I have tried to stop my risky sex, but have not been able to. 2 1

IV. Risk – TOTAL = _____

	LIKE ME	UNLIKE ME

Related to my sexual addiction...

Afterwards, I feel guilty about what I have done. 2 1

I am ashamed to admit to anyone about my sexual behavior. 2 1

My shame makes my life more painful. 2 1

I feel helpless about changing my behavior. 2 1

I hate myself after engaging in unhealthy sex behavior. 2 1

V. Emotions – TOTAL = _____

Scoring Directions

The *Escaping Emotional Pain Assessment* is designed to measure the severity of your emotional pain and how, if left unchecked, it can lead to additional excessive sexual habits.

In the five sections on the previous pages, count the scores you circled for each of the items. Put that total on the line marked "Total" at the end of each section. Transfer your totals to the spaces below:

I.	Pain Total	_____
II.	Escape Total	_____
III.	Action Total	_____
IV.	Risk Total	_____
V.	Emotions Total	_____

(Continue on the next page for the scale descriptions and profile interpretations)

Escaping Emotional Pain Assessment

Scale Descriptions & Profile Interpretation

In each of the sections, place an X on the line to note your score:

SCALE I – Pain – (This scale measures the amount of emotional pain you are experiencing.)

5 = Low	8 = Moderate	10 = High

SCALE II – Escape – (This scale measures how much you rely on sex as an escape.)

5 = Low	8 = Moderate	10 = High

SCALE III – Action – (This scale measures how regularly you engage in excessive sexual behaviors.)

5 = Low	8 = Moderate	10 = High

SCALE IV – Risk – (This scale measures the amount of risk you are putting yourself and others through.)

5 = Low	8 = Moderate	10 = High

SCALE V – Emotions – (This scale measures the impact of your emotions after engaging in unhealthy sexual behaviors.)

5 = Low	8 = Moderate	10 = High

Remember that even one "LIKE ME" score on any of the scales can suggest you are experiencing emotional effects from a sexual addiction. Areas in which you scored LOW suggest that you are not experiencing many signs of a sexual addiction in those areas. The HIGHER your score on each of the scales, the more of a sex-related problem you have in the specific aspect measured by the assessment.

Unpleasant Experiences

Many people use sexual behavior to escape from their emotional pain. They are prone to dwell on unpleasant or disappointing experiences in life. Some of these experiences are real and some are imagined, but they take their toll on one's well-being. When this occurs, many people look for an escape through sexual acts.

In the boxes below, identify some of the unpleasant and disappointing experiences in your life. Next to each box, write about how you have reacted to those experiences.

My Unpleasant Experieinces

My Emotions

An important aspect of developing and utilizing emotional strength and dealing with emotional pain is to begin to develop a deep awareness of your own emotions.

As the day goes on today, keep this paper with you, notice your emotions, and write them in Darwin's "The Expressions of the Emotions in Man and Animals" categories below:

Suffering and weeping	Low spirits, anxiety, grief, dejection, despair
Reflection, meditation, determination	Joy, high spirits, love, tender feelings, devotion
Hatred and anger	Disdain, contempt, disgust, guilt, pride, and negation
Surprise, astonishment, fear, horror	Self-attention, shame, shyness, modesty, blushing

On the lines below, journal about what you learned about your everyday emotions by separating them.

_____

_____

_____

Express Your Emotions

People who are addicted to sexual behaviors experience a lot of emotions, and find it difficult to identify them.

Journal about your feelings right now regarding your sexual behaviors. Don't filter your thoughts, just write!

_____

_____

_____

_____

_____

_____

_____

_____

_____

_____

Draw your feelings right now regarding your sexual behaviors. Don't filter your thoughts, just draw!

What Do My Emotions Mean?

Resist the impulse to ignore your unpleasant feelings, push them away, or judge them. Instead, think about what they are trying to tell you. All emotions, especially the most difficult ones, exist to provide you with information.

Below, explore the unpleasant emotions you experience before, during, and after unhealthy sexual behavior, and try to determine what the emotions really mean.

My Emotion	How I Experience It	What it Means
Example: Anger at my partner.	*I get a headache.*	*I wish JID was more attuned to my needs.*

We're all emotional beings; once we wholeheartedly accept this and deepen our emotional literacy, we make more room for meeting one another in ever-richer, more relationally rewarding ways.
~Robert Augustus Masters, PhD

My Shame

Hidden shame often drives psychological symptoms such as anger, rage, and avoidance, as well as self-destructive behaviors like excessive, unhealthy sex. These self-destructive behaviors are an attempt to regulate the overpowering, painful feelings but actually lead to more shame, hiding and secrecy, propelling the self-destructive cycle.

Below, identify the feelings being driven by your shame, your self-destructive sexual behaviors, and how you react to shame. Look at this example and then you try filling in the large blocks below.

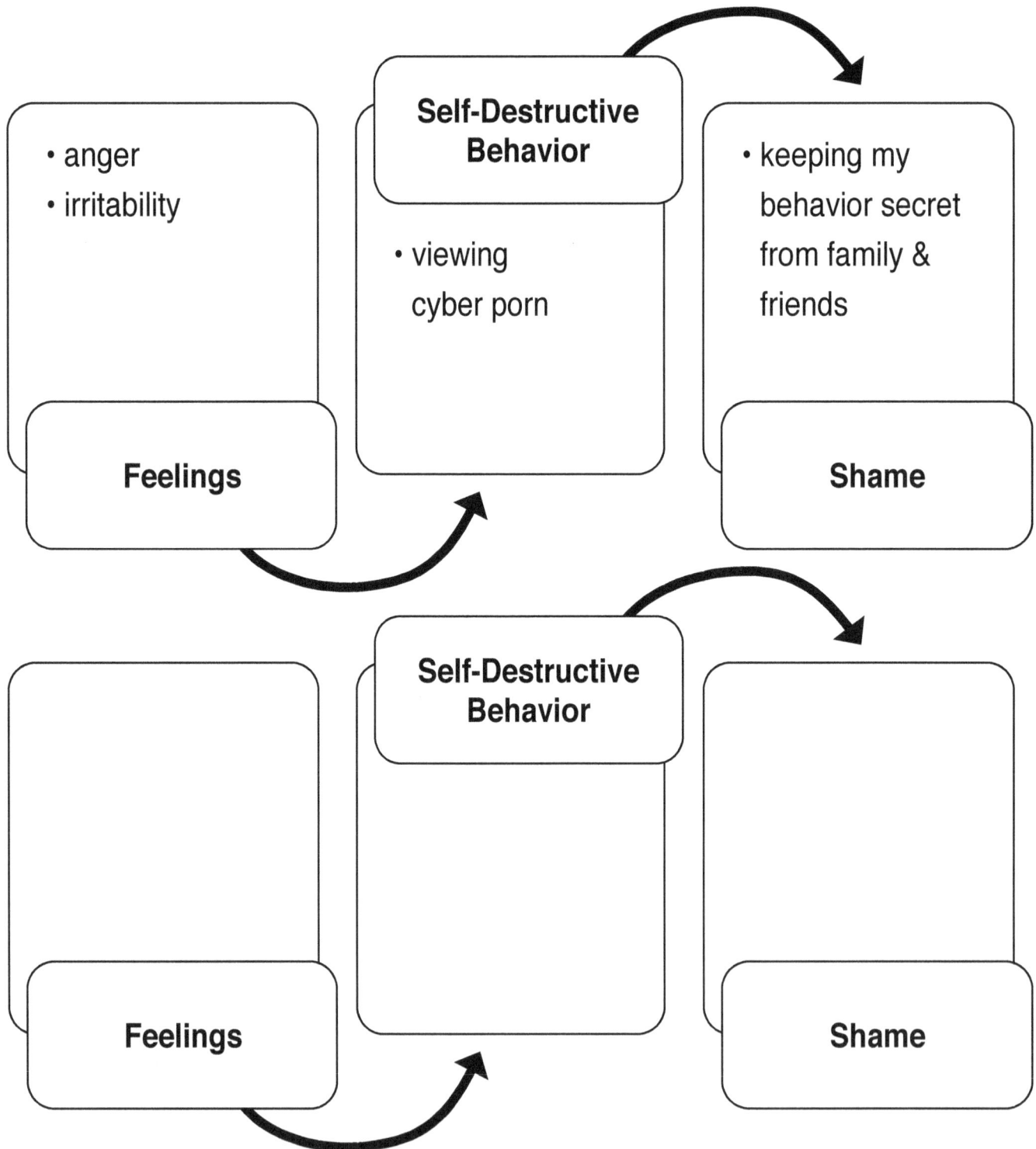

Self-Destructive Behavior

- anger
- irritability

- viewing cyber porn

- keeping my behavior secret from family & friends

Feelings

Shame

Self-Destructive Behavior

Feelings

Shame

The Antidote to Shame

One of the best ways to overcome the shame of a sex addiction is to take actions that generate pride in yourself. This may include going to college for a degree, starting a business, getting a promotion at work, planting a garden, or cleaning the house. The actions can be large or small, but they will generate a sense of pride in yourself, and occupy your time and energy. This will allow you to think less about sex, and to act on your thoughts even less.

In the spaces that follow, identify four actions that can act as an antidote to shame.

#1	#2

#3	#4

Break Your Secrecy

Other people can help you deal with the emotions and the emotional pain you are experiencing. One way to ensure this is by breaking your secrecy with someone who will understand. It can be a family member, friend, a mental health therapist, or anyone you trust.

Who are these people in your life? **USE NAME CODES.**

List the people, how you can tell them about your secret, and how will this disclosure can help you.

Person: *HFL*

> *Ex.: At a quiet place for dinner, I can explain, and ask for his suggestions.*

Person:

Person:

Person:

Person:

Tune into Your Feelings

People who turn to sexual behavior rather than dealing with their emotions are often unaware of their emotions or how they are experiencing them. It is important to learn to name the emotions you are experiencing by listening to your mind and body and to understand what they are trying to tell you.

Ways Feelings Are Experienced	My Feelings	How I Experience this Feeling	What it is Trying to Tell Me
Example: My body	*Irritability with my children.*	*My heart pounds.*	*Slow down, step back, and take some deep breaths.*
Body			
Example: Thoughts & Beliefs	*Depression.*	*I keep thinking I am not good enough.*	*Reflect on worthwhile things I have done.*
Thoughts & Beliefs			
Example: Actions	*Shame after unprotected sex.*	*I feel bad for days after my encounters.*	*Find ways to channel my sexual energy.*
Actions			

When you begin to feel an emotion such as worthlessness, resentment, emptiness, shame, or loneliness, feel it completely rather than avoid or suppress it. This means allowing the feelings to arise in the body and notice the sensations that occur. Don't manipulate or try to control them. Allow yourself to be present and observe them. Remember to ask, "What is this emotion trying to tell me?"

Use Your Pain for Good

Sometimes you can channel your emotional pain to help others. Rather than focusing on your pain and using sex as a release, try thinking of ways you can use your circumstances to improve your own life and the lives of others.

What are some of the ways you can channel negative emotions into something positive?

Ways I Could Help	Opportunity Options	How This Would Help Others and Me, Too!
Example: Help people	*During the time I would usually have a sexual interaction, I could volunteer in the homeless shelter in my community.*	*It would provide an outlet for me to use my excess energy, while helping people in need. I could talk with friends and inspire them to join me at the shelter.*

Helping others is a great way to help yourself!

Self-Compassion

Being kind to yourself is essential for overcoming emotional pain. When addicted to sex, you are often your own worst critic and beat yourself up when you fail to try to stop. Instead, it is important to show yourself loving kindness and compassion. Self-compassion will allow you to move from shame and guilt to forgiveness, and hopefully to live your life in a healthier and more beneficial way.

Ways To Show Myself Self-Compassion	How I Can Show Myself Self-Compassion
Accept yourself for who you are	
Forgive yourself	
Engage in activities that are soothing and comforting rather than unhealthy sexual behaviors	
Reward yourself when you are able to abstain	
Repeat positive affirmations to yourself	
Give yourself permission to be less than perfect	
Eat and sleep healthfully	
Share with others	
Compliment yourself when you deserve it	
Reward yourself with a spa or gym day	
Other	
Other	

Feeling compassion for ourselves in no way releases us from responsibility for our actions. Rather, it releases us from the self-hatred that prevents us from responding to our life with clarity and balance.
~ Tara Brach

Emotional Coping

To be more successful in coping with your unpleasant emotions, you can use many effective techniques.

Place a check mark in the box in front of the coping activities you have tried in the past, and write about the effects of this practice. Underline the coping techniques you will make a commitment to do!

☐ **Yoga.**

_____

_____

☐ **Tai chi.**

_____

_____

☐ **Mindfulness.**

_____

_____

☐ **Soothing music.**

_____

_____

☐ **Deep breaths.**

_____

_____

☐ **Meditation and/or prayer.**

_____

_____

☐ **Support groups for people who have an addiction.**

_____

_____

☐ **Make an appointment with a therapist to learn social skills, boundary setting, assertiveness, etc.**

_____

_____

☐ **Other coping techniques that have worked for you in the past.**

_____

_____

Loss & Grief

Feelings of loss and unresolved grief can be an emotional trigger for sex addicts. This loss can be the loss of a loved one, loss of a pet, or loss of a way of life. When you are unable to deal with your grief from a loss, it can negatively affect you for a long time. Some people use their addiction to "feel better" but that is only temporary!

My loss was...

_____

_____

_____

This loss affected me by...

_____

_____

_____

I can't seem to get over this loss because...

_____

_____

_____

The emotions I am constantly feeling are...

_____

_____

_____

I wish I could have...

_____

_____

_____

To move on I need to...

_____

_____

_____

I would like to...

_____

_____

_____

I can go to _____ *for healthy, wise, kind support.*
                      (use name code)

Feeling Good About Myself

Low self-esteem can prolong your emotional pain and damage your emotional health. Once your self-esteem starts to dip, it will usually lead to sexual urges. Completion of these sexual urges will make you feel better about yourself, but only temporarily. Then, guilt, shame, other relationships, and real life set in.

Think about all of the things that you like about yourself and that make you feel good. Then, build on them.

Things I Like About Myself	How I Will Build on Them
Example: I am smart and I make friends easily.	*I might look for a job where I can sell things and use my personality type to my advantage.*

Ways to Increase Your Self-Esteem

✔ Get outside and into nature.
✔ Picture your future self as you want you to be: then make it happen.
✔ Take time out from social media and volunteer to help people.
✔ Avoid comparing yourself to other people—be yourself.
✔ Give yourself a break and be kind to yourself.
✔ Replace negative thoughts about yourself with more positive ones.
✔ Be assertive and tell people what you need in life.
✔ Set goals that will keep you focused on things other than sex.

A Trauma in My Life – Page 1

A trauma can create feelings that often trigger urges to engage in unhealthy sexual behavior.

Think about a trauma you experienced in the past. Journaling about that experience can help you make sense of the event, reduce your distress, and let go of the need to engage in excessive, unhealthy sex.

Before you begin...

1. *Find a quiet time and place where there are few distractions.*
2. *Don't be concerned if there is background noise or if you have only a short period of time.*
3. *Take a few minutes to think about how your traumatic event has impacted you and your life.*
4. *Begin writing about your deepest thoughts and feelings regarding the traumatic event you experienced.*

What were you doing before the event? _____

_____

_____

What happened?_____

_____

_____

What did you do? _____

_____

_____

What didn't you do? _____

_____

_____

What ways did it change your life? _____

_____

_____

What, if anything, could you have done differently? _____

_____

_____

What do you remember about the event that stays with you? _____

_____

_____

(Continued on the next page)

A Trauma in My Life – Page 2

How did you know it was over? _____

_____

What did you do after it was over? _____

_____

In what ways has the event changed your life? _____

_____

In what ways did it change your relationship with friends? _____

_____

In what ways did it change your relationship with family members? _____

_____

How has the event affected your future? _____

_____

What was the worst aspect of the ordeal? _____

_____

Who do you blame for what happened? _____

_____

How do you blame yourself? _____

_____

What are your thoughts about the event after responding to these questions? _____

_____

Quotes about Escaping Emotional Pain

On the lines that follow each of the quotes, describe what the quote means to you and how it applies to YOUR life.

You are loved just for being who you are, just for existing. You don't have to do anything to earn it. Your shortcomings, your lack of self-esteem, physical perfection, or social and economic success – none of that matters. No one can take this love away from you, and it will always be here.
~ Ram Dass

_____

_____

_____

Love who you are, embrace who you are. Love yourself. When you love yourself, people can kind of pick up on that: they can see confidence, they can see self-esteem, and naturally, people gravitate towards you.
~ Lilly Singh

_____

_____

_____

Shame is the most powerful, master emotion. It's the fear that we're not good enough.
~ Brene Brown

_____

_____

_____

Which quote especially speaks to you about escaping emotional pain? Why?

_____

_____

_____

_____

© 2021 WHOLE PERSON ASSOCIATES, 101 WEST 2ND STREET, SUITE 203, DULUTH MN 55802 • 800-247-6789 • WHOLEPERSON.COM

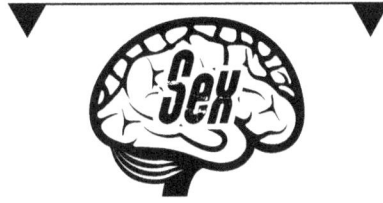

Loss of Control

Name _____

Date _____

Loss of Control Assessment
Introduction and Directions

Sex addiction is primarily marked by a loss of control where people can no longer control the compulsion to have sex, despite experiencing many negative consequences. The Loss of Control Assessment was designed to help you explore the ways one is able to control, or not control, sexual-related impulses.

This assessment contains 15 statements related to various ways that sex and sex-related behaviors can make personal control difficult.

Read each statement and decide whether or not the statement describes you. If the statement is TRUE, circle the number next to that item under the "True" column. If the statement is FALSE, circle the number next to that item under the "FALSE" column.

In the example below, the circled number 2 under "TRUE"
indicates the statement is true about the person completing the individual scale.

	TRUE	FALSE
When it comes to sexual behavior...		
I am constantly thinking about sex.	(2)	1

This is not a test. Since there are no right or wrong answers, do not spend too much time thinking about your answers. Be sure to respond to every statement. Be Honest!

(Turn to the next page and begin.)

Loss of Control Assessment

Name _____ Date _____

---------- **PREOCCUPATION SCALE** ----------

	TRUE	FALSE

When it comes to sexual behavior...

I am constantly thinking about sex. 2 1

I fantasize about sex when not engaging in it. 2 1

I have sexual urges throughout the day. 2 1

I feel like my sexual urges are a major focus of my life. 2 1

I feel driven toward certain sexual behaviors. 2 1

Preoccupation Scale – TOTAL = _____

---------- **ESCALATION SCALE** ----------

	TRUE	FALSE

When it comes to sexual behavior...

I am now using sex to escape from my daily life. 2 1

I notice that my sexual needs are increasing. 2 1

I am engaging in some type of sex more often than ever. 2 1

I need more and more sexual gratification as time goes on. 2 1

I am now leading a double life. 2 1

Escalation Scale – TOTAL = _____

---------- **CONTROL SCALE** ----------

	TRUE	FALSE

When it comes to sexual behavior...

I feel as if my sexual life is no longer in my control. 2 1

I have been unsuccessful in controlling my sexual fantasies. 2 1

I can no longer manage my sexual impulses. 2 1

I feel helpless to change my actions despite the negative consequences. 2 1

I am completely out of control. 2 1

Control Scale – TOTAL = _____

(Continued on the next page)

© 2021 WHOLE PERSON ASSOCIATES, 101 WEST 2ND STREET, SUITE 203, DULUTH MN 55802 • 800-247-6789 • WHOLEPERSON.COM

Loss of Control Assessment
Scoring & Profile Interpretations

The assessment you just completed views the effects of sexual activity on various aspects of your life.

On the previous pages, add the scores you circled and put that number in the line marked TOTAL. Transfer that number below. Place each number on the continuum line of the matching Scale below:

Preoccupation Scale
(This scale measures the extent to which sex takes up your time and energy each day.)

_____
5 = Low   8 = Moderate   10 = High

Escalation Scale
(This scale measures the extent to which the need for sex is staying the same or accelerating.)

_____
5 = Low   8 = Moderate   10 = High

Control Scale
(This scale measures the extent of which your sexual-related behavior is in or out of control.)

_____
5 = Low   8 = Moderate   10 = High

The higher your score in any of the scales, the greater risk you have for experiencing negative effects of sexual behavior. However, by circling even ONE Medium or High answer, you can be at risk for experiencing negative effects on your personal and/or professional life.

Sex as an Escape

People with a sex addiction are often preoccupied with sex, and use it as an escape mechanism from their problems, stressors, and feelings.

In each section below, write about, doodle, or draw your escape issues.

I try to escape loneliness by …	**I try to escape sadness by …**
I try to escape anxiety by …	**I try to escape stress by …**
I try to escape _____ by …	**I try to escape _____ by …**

When all the routines and details and the human bores get on our nerves, we just yearn to go away from here to somewhere else. To go fishing is a sound, a valid, and an accepted reason for an escape. It requires no explanation.

~ Herbert Hoover

What else can you do to "go away from here to somewhere else" without involving sex?

_____

_____

_____

_____

Impulse Journal

A critical component in learning how to control impulses is to be aware of how often those impulses occur. This can help you realize just how often you are getting sexual urges as well as how you can maintain self-control rather than acting impulsively.

For one week, keep a log of your sex-related urges and how you showed or didn't show self-control. Reproduce this form to use as often as needed.

Days	My Urge ...	How I showed, or didn't show, self-control.
Example: Monday	*I wanted to go to my partner during lunch hour for a quickie.*	*I decided not to go because I would never be back in time.*
Example: Monday	*I wanted to go to my partner during lunch hour for a quickie.*	*I went and didn't get back in time. I was given notice of one more time and I'm fired.*
Monday		
Tuesday		
Wednesday		
Thursday		
Friday		
Saturday		
Sunday		

Impulse Control Problems

It is important to recognize and assess the areas of your life in which a lack of impulse control has caused problems.

Below, journal about the ways your lack of impulse control has led to unhealthy, excessive sexual behaviors that have interfered with various aspects of your life.

Areas of My Life	How My Life Has Been Affected	How I Could Show Restraint
Example: *Work Life*	*I am up late at night and I am impatient, grumpy, and ineffective at my job.*	*Give up watching porn late at night when everyone else is sleeping. Maybe start a good television series with the family and then go to bed.*
Work Life		
Relationships		
School		
Finances		
Emotions		
Community		
Legal Issues		
Other		

What does this Kazi Shams quote mean to you? "One's greatest challenge is to control oneself."

_____

_____

How will you accept the challenge of impulse control and do something about it?

_____

_____

My Early Warning System

Even though impulsive urges lead to long-term problems, they can serve a purpose for you. They trigger a need to cope with emotional pain in some way. These urges are your warning system! You have your choice as to how to cope with that pain! One way of preventing impulsive behaviors is finding a different, healthier behavior that can serve that same purpose.

Healthy Behaviors That Could Replace Impulse Behaviors

In the box before each sentence, check the items that you are currently using when you get a sexual urge. In the line after the items that you are willing to try, write when you will start.

☐ Add humor to a stressful situation. _____

☐ Be creative—music, art, garden. _____

☐ Confide in someone you trust. _____

☐ Develop a support network. _____

☐ Do a crossword puzzle or Sudoku. _____

☐ Engage in a healthy hobby. _____

☐ Enjoy your healthy relationships. _____

☐ Escape from reality by reading. _____

☐ Exercise at the gym or outside. _____

☐ Explore ways to relax. _____

☐ Find or begin a support group. _____

☐ Go outside and enjoy nature. _____

☐ Identify your negative thinking and reframe. _____

☐ Journal about your feelings. _____

☐ Keep a journal of unusual or scary thoughts or behaviors. _____

☐ Listen to music. _____

☐ Maintain friends who listen and support. _____

☐ Meditate, attend a house of worship, and/or talk with a spiritual leader. _____

☐ Punch a punching bag. _____

☐ Make an appointment with a professional to talk about your issues. _____

☐ Repeat positive self-affirmations. _____

☐ Sing, play an instrument, and/or dance. _____

☐ Take time for yourself to enjoy healthy activities. _____

☐ Think about your blessings and appreciate them. _____

☐ Walk or hike. _____

☐ Write your story. _____

☐ Other: _____

☐ Other: _____

☐ Other: _____

☐ Other: _____

Loss of Control Case Study

> SKL has trouble controlling compulsive sexual urges.
> SKL thinks of sex all the time, and it is interfering with work.
> SKL will start to think about a sexual fantasy and cannot stop.
> In addition, SKL has lost friends and a partner's trust.
> SKL is also worried that unsafe sexual behavior may lead to health problems.

What is SKL's primary problem?

_____

_____

_____

What is a way that SKL can stop compulsive urges?

_____

_____

_____

What can SKL do when starting to fantasize?

_____

_____

_____

What should SKL do?

_____

_____

_____

What advice would you give to SKL?

_____

_____

_____

Is this similar to anything in your life? Explain.

_____

_____

_____

If this is similar to your story, what can you do?

_____

_____

_____

Be Mindful

Being aware and attentive of your unpleasant feelings, urges, impulses, and desires in a non-judgmental manner, by noticing them without attaching to them in a mindful manner, can be very helpful to people addicted to sex. By doing this, they are able to notice their thoughts and acknowledge them, and watch as they float away or dissolve.

Below are two different ways to be mindful when you begin to feel sexual urges and impulses:

Start Now by Following This Script

- Close your eyes and concentrate on your breathing.
- Thoughts will pop into your head and attempt to distract your concentration on your breathing.
- Try not to get distracted by your thoughts, simply notice them and let them pass by.
- What do you hear?
- What do you smell?
- What do you sense?
- Pay attention to how you feel while doing this. How do you feel physically? Emotionally?
- Think of nothing else until the urge goes away.

What do you notice after you have completed this activity?

_____

_____

_____

Mindful Minute-of-Breathing Script

- When you begin to feel an unsafe or unhealthy urge coming on, lower your eyes and notice the air going in and out at your nostrils or the rise and fall of your chest or stomach.
- If you can't feel anything, place your hand on your stomach and notice how your hand gently rises and falls with your breath.
- As you start to notice your breath, start to lengthen the in-breath and the out-breath.
- Concentrate completely on your breathing until the urge goes away.
- Remember, just because you have an impulse does not mean you have to act on it!

What do you notice after you have completed this activity?

_____

_____

_____

The present moment is filled with joy and happiness.
If you are attentive, you will see it.
~ Thich Nhat Hanh

A Self-Discipline Quotation

Self-discipline is about controlling your desires and impulses while
staying focused on what needs to get done to achieve your goal.
~ Adam Sicinski

What does this quote say to you regarding your present sexual behaviors?

_____

_____

_____

How can you be more self-disciplined when it comes to your unhealthy sexual behaviors?

_____

_____

_____

How are you currently controlling your sexual impulses and desires?

_____

_____

_____

How could you do a better job of controlling your sexual impulses and desires?

_____

_____

_____

What is a goal on which you need to stay focused?

_____

_____

_____

What will achieving this goal mean for you personally and professionally?

_____

_____

_____

© 2021 WHOLE PERSON ASSOCIATES, 101 WEST 2ND STREET, SUITE 203, DULUTH MN 55802 • 800-247-6789 • WHOLEPERSON.COM

Social Engineering

It is important to be prepared for your sexual urges. Preparing can help you develop a plan to keep your urges under control. You need to keep visual stimuli and anything that might trigger a sexual urge out of your everyday environment. This is called social engineering and it can very helpful!

Think of some ways you can alter your environment to help you cope better with impulse control. This approach can help you learn to manage sexual urges in a safe and healthy way by managing your environment in better ways.

Possible Triggers of a Sexual Urge	How I Will Avoid The Triggers	The Result
Example: My House	*I will no longer subscribe to television channels that have explicit sexual content.*	*I will watch more wholesome programming and be less stimulated.*
My House		
My Friends		
My Family		
My Time		
My Electronics		
My Entertainment		
My Social Life		
Other		
Other		

Distract Yourself

Urges to engage in impulsive sexual behaviors may be very strong and make it very difficult to cope. If not acted upon, these urges will usually pass fairly quickly. If you can distract yourself when you experience an urge, you may be able to outsmart the urge and just let it pass.

**Below are a number of healthy distraction strategies that may be helpful
in riding out a strong urge or an unpleasant emotional experience.**

- Have another activity or hobby to immediately engage your attention.
- Distract yourself with exercise or physical activity.
- Stop isolating yourself and spend more time with others.
- Quickly go into a mindfulness meditation in which you focus on clearing your mind, becoming aware of your surroundings, and maybe even chanting a phrase like "I will not give in!"
- Do something creative like reading, journaling, pottery, or drawing.

*Begin your creativity by drawing the responses to the sentence starters below.
(Stick figures are okay!)*

When I get a sexual urge I will …

When I get a sexual urge I will not …

How Much Control Do You Have?

Many people with a sexual addiction are unaware of their ability to control their sexual urges, and unaware of their lack of ability to control their sexual urges.

On the line under each example of the ability to control sexual urges, place an X on the continuum of how much you relate to the statement. On the dotted line below each one, write why you rated yourself that way. Be HONEST!

I can control the fantasies in my mind.

0 (Not Like Me)   5 (Somewhat Like Me)   10 (Much Like Me)

. . . .

I can control sexual urges by distracting myself.

0 (Not Like Me)   5 (Somewhat Like Me)   10 (Much Like Me)

. . . .

I can stop engaging in unhealthy sex whenever I want.

0 (Not Like Me)   5 (Somewhat Like Me)   10 (Much Like Me)

. . . .

I am not really addicted to sex.

0 (Not Like Me)   5 (Somewhat Like Me)   10 (Much Like Me)

. . . .

It's other people's fault that I am the way I am.

0 (Not Like Me)   5 (Somewhat Like Me)   10 (Much Like Me)

. . . .

I am aware of the consequences of my sexual addiction.

0 (Not Like Me)   5 (Somewhat Like Me)   10 (Much Like Me)

. . . .

I feel helpless to stop my sexual urges.

0 (Not Like Me)   5 (Somewhat Like Me)   10 (Much Like Me)

. . . .

My Positive Skills

Most people have positive skills that can divert the focus and get rid of negative thoughts to use control when unhealthy or unsafe sexual urges or triggers occur. Look back over your life and find some positive things in your past or present.

Name the positive people (USE NAME CODES), accomplishments, successes, hobbies, etc., that have provided you with positives in your life and describe how you can leverage these positives to resist your sexual urges.

Positives in My Life

Example: M.E.A. always told me that I have the ability to accomplish anything I really wanted to.

How I Can Use This Positive

Example: I can work on overcoming my sexual addiction. I have proved her right before and I can do it again!

What Do I Need in a Relationship?

Thriving in caring, supportive relationships can keep you satisfied emotionally, promote contentment, and help you to resist unhealthy, unsafe sexual urges. If you get what you truly need in your relationships, you may not have the need to resort to "quick fixes."

Types of Relationships	Name Codes	How I Get (or Don't Get) What I Need	What More Can I Do in the Future?
Intimate	JTA	She is a wonderful partner in every other aspect of our lives but sex. She has a different sex-drive and different needs than I do. I am embarrassed to discuss it with her. I don't want her to feel bad.	I can tell her that I have a problem and would like to talk with her and a therapist or trusted friend who might be helpful.
Intimate			
Familial			
Friendships			
Neighbors			
Co-Workers			
Acquaintances			
Other			

How can you be more assertive in asking for what you need?

_____

_____

My Impulsive Urges

Think about what happens when you act on your sexual urges without being able to control them.

Respond to the sentence starters to learn more about yourself and your behavior. Use name codes.

When I act on my impulsive sexual urges, I _____

_____

When I act on my impulsive sexual urges, I am unable to_____

_____

When I act on my impulsive sexual urges, my friends _____

_____

When I act on my impulsive sexual urges, my family members_____

_____

When I act on my impulsive sexual urges, I avoid _____

_____

When I act on my impulsive sexual urges, I often _____

_____

When I act on my impulsive sexual urges, my self-esteem_____

_____

When I act on my impulsive sexual urges, I experience negative consequences such as _____

_____

When I act on my impulsive sexual urges, I feel _____

_____

Negative Consequences

Most people who have an addiction are driven by the short-term false rewards of their behaviors. They usually repeat behaviors that work well at the moment, regardless of the long-term negative consequences. It is important to increase your awareness of the long-term negative consequences of your unhealthy and/or unsafe sexual behaviors.

Identify the short-term and long-term pros and cons of your unhealthy sexual behaviors.

My Unhealthy and/or Unsafe Sexual Behaviors	Pros of the Behavior	Cons of the Behavior
Example: Masturbate after viewing online pornography when everyone in the house goes to sleep.	*I am not exposed to partners with HIV/Aids.*	*Fear of my spouse or kids walking in on me.*

Getting Back in Touch

In trying to get away from unpleasant emotions, people addicted to sex often use sexual behavior as a poor coping mechanism rather than coping in a healthy, responsible way.

Use the following 5 steps as a way of coping with sexual urges:

Step 1: Identify the sexual behavior that needs to be changed.

Step 2: Identify what happens prior to the sexual behavior.

Step 3: Explore your thoughts and feelings at the time.

Step 4: Identify what your thoughts and feelings pushed you to do.

Step 5: Consider the consequences that occurred.

Think back to the last time you engaged in a poor coping method of unhealthy or unsafe sexual behavior and answer the questions from the above coping model.

Step 1: What was the sexual behavior in which you engaged and what needed to change?

_____

_____

Step 2: What happened prior to the sexual behavior?

_____

_____

Step 3: What thoughts and feelings did you experience at that time?

_____

_____

Step 4: What did your thoughts and feelings push you to do?

_____

_____

Step 5: What were the consequences that occurred?

_____

_____

Quotes about Controlling Sexual Impulses

*On the lines that follow each of the quotes,
describe what they mean to you and how they apply to YOUR life.*

It would be impossible to estimate how much time and energy we invest in trying to fix, change and deny our emotions - especially the ones that shake us at our very core, like hurt, jealousy, loneliness, shame, rage and grief.
~ Debbie Ford

_____

_____

Personal health is related to self-control and to the worship of life in all its natural beauty - self-control bringing with it happiness, renewed youth, and long life.
~ Maria Montessori

_____

_____

Self-control is one mark of a mature person; it applies to control of language, physical treatment of others, and the appetites of the body.
~ Joseph B. Wirthlin

_____

_____

Emotional self-control is the result of hard work, not an inherent skill.
~ Travis Bradberry

_____

_____

Which quote especially speaks to you and your sexual addiction? Why?

_____

_____

_____

_____

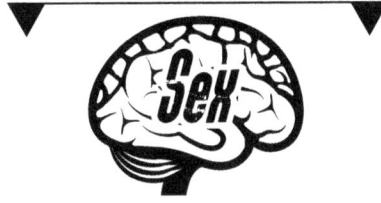

A Hopeful Future

Name _____

Date _____

A Hopeful Future Assessment
Introduction and Directions

An important aspect of a recovery process for people dealing with a sexual addiction is planning for a hopeful and productive future. You can start this process today by making a conscientious effort to reduce and ultimately eliminate negative and unsafe sexual activity and begin living a positive, safe, productive life.

The following assessment contains 18 statements related to your future plans and goals. This assessment can help you to gauge your level of readiness to move on to a bright, hopeful future.

Read each of the statements and decide whether or not the statement describes you.

If the statement describes you, circle the number in the YES column next to that item.
If the statement does not describe you, circle the number in the NO column next to that item.

In the following example, the circled 2 indicates that the person completing this assessment does not believe that the statement describes them:

	YES	NO
I am satisfied with the way my life is going right now.	1	(2)

This is not a test. Since there are no right or wrong answers, do not spend too much time thinking about your answers. Be sure to respond to every statement.

(Turn to the next page and begin.)

A Hopeful Future Assessment

Name _____ Date _____

	YES	NO
I am satisfied with the way my life is going right now.	1	2
I have forgiven myself for mistakes and shortcomings.	2	1
I am not able to find satisfaction in simple, everyday pleasures.	1	2
I have an optimistic outlook in life.	2	1
I see setbacks as opportunities for growth.	2	1
I rarely take responsibility for my life.	1	2

Hope – TOTAL = _____

	YES	NO
I am not getting closer to achieving my dreams.	1	2
I feel supported in achieving my goals.	2	1
I am making progress toward goals important to me.	2	1
I am not as productive as I want to be.	1	2
I want to start taking responsibility for my actions.	2	1
I have set long-range goals for my success.	2	1

Productivity – TOTAL = _____

	YES	NO
I rarely think about the future.	1	2
I am hopeful about the future.	2	1
I rarely make plans ahead of time.	1	2
I am sure that eventually good things will happen in my future.	2	1
I do not think my future looks very bright.	1	2
I am hopeful that the future will bring me many opportunities.	2	1

Future – TOTAL = _____

*Go to the next page for scoring assessment
results, profile interpretation, and individual descriptions.*

A Hopeful Future Assessment

Scoring Directions & Profile Interpretations

The assessment you just completed is designed to measure your interest in creating a more hopeful future.

For each of the sections on the previous page, count the scores you circled. Put that total on the line marked TOTAL at the end of each section. Transfer your total to the space below.

HOPE Total = _____

PRODUCTIVITY Total = _____

FUTURE Total = _____

~~~~~~

Assessment Profile Interpretation

Individual Scale Scores	Results	Indications
6 to 7 in any single area	Low	Low scores indicate that you may lack some readiness to begin creating a bright, hopeful future.
8 to 10 in any single area	Moderate	Moderate scores indicate that you are somewhat ready to begin creating a bright, hopeful future.
11 to 12 in any single area	High	High scores indicate that you are definitely ready to begin creating a bright, hopeful future.

HOPE—People scoring high on this scale are not satisfied with how their lives are going, and are ready to take action for a better future.

PRODUCTIVITY—People scoring high on this scale are ready to be proactive, set goals, and take responsibility in reaching these goals.

FUTURE—People scoring high on this scale are interested in planning for, and working toward a better future.

Being More Accountable

In order to begin to create the future you desire, you need to be more accountable for your actions, rather than making excuses for them. It is important to recognize that overcoming a sex addiction is within your power to control. Once you own a problem, you are on your way to solving it!

Think about what is in your control and hold yourself responsible for those things within your control. In the circles below, identify the ways you can and will be more accountable.

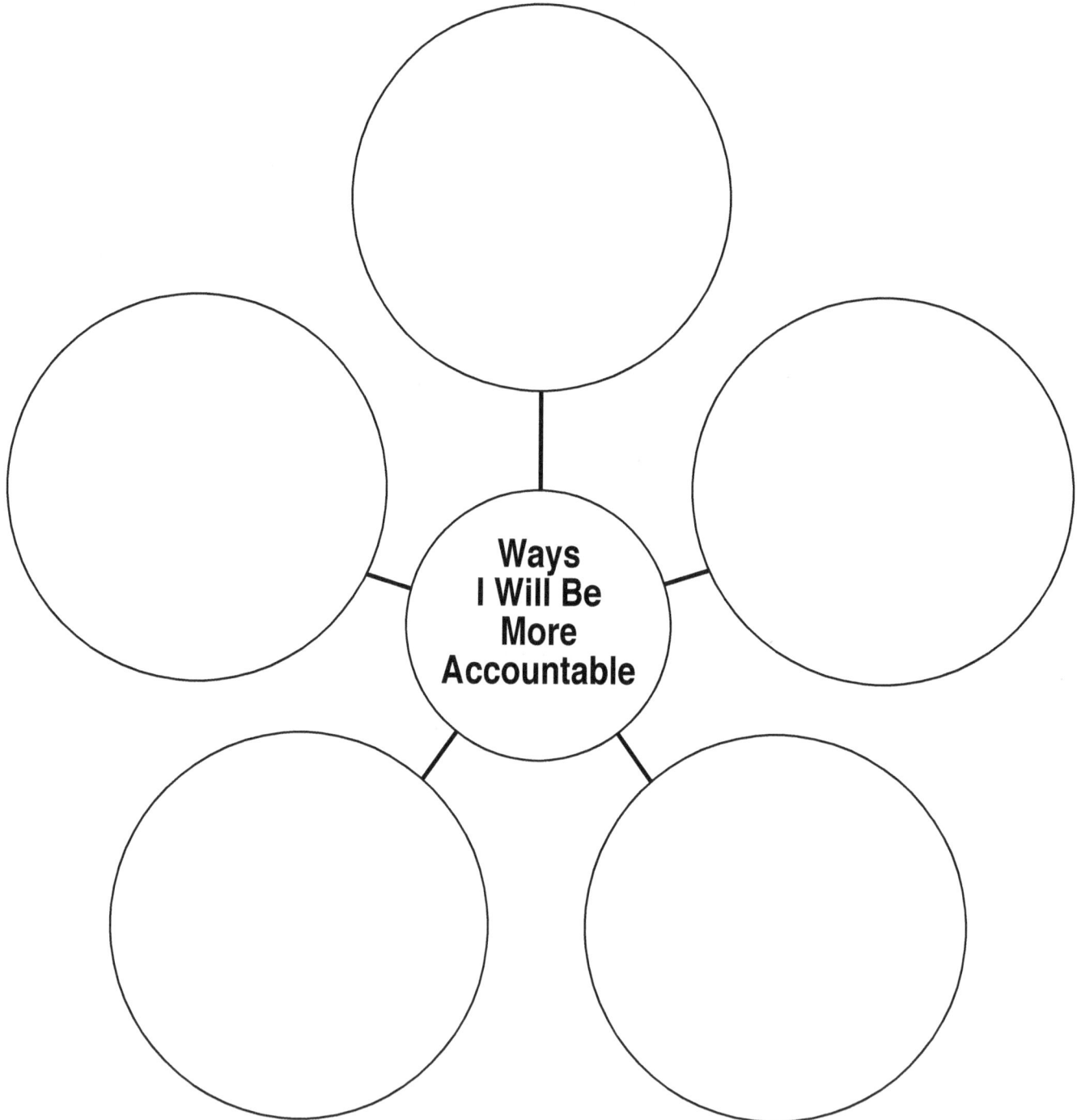

Ways I Will Be More Accountable

It is not only what we do, but also what we do not do, for which we are accountable.
~ Moliere

Being More Productive

People who are successful in overcoming a sex addiction are able to control their thoughts and action to the extent that they want to do something more productive than engaging in unsafe and unhealthy sexual behaviors.

Below, explore how you can become more productive.

Thoughts	Actions I Need to Take	How I Can Be More Productive
Example: I know I am neglecting my chores around our home.	*I need to take care of my responsibilities.*	*I can make a list of things to do each day, and do them, no matter what!*

Ways to Be More Productive

- Follow the 80/20 rule. Only 20 percent of what you do each day produces 80 percent of your results. Eliminate the things that don't matter in your life because they have a minimal effect on your overall productivity.
- Focus on one goal at a time rather than multi-tasking.
- Identify and utilize your most productive times of the workday.
- Make a reasonable to-do list each day.
- Set small goals for your tasks and focus on one goal at a time.

Practice Gratitude

Being grateful, even for small things, can help boost your mood and self-esteem in significant ways.

Identify five things and five people in your life for which you are grateful, and describe why.

Things	**People**
	USE NAME CODES

1. _____

2. _____

3. _____

4. _____

5. _____

1. _____

2. _____

3. _____

4. _____

5. _____

Ways to Express Gratitude

- Practice gratitude by repeating thankfulness mantras such as, "I am thankful for positive people and activities in my life."
- Keep a gratitude journal in which you continue to write about all of the positive aspects of your life for which you are grateful.
- Express gratitude toward the people for whom you are grateful. Let them know what you appreciate about them.
- Perform a random act of kindness toward someone for whom you are grateful.
- Perform a random act of kindness toward someone you do not know, just because you are grateful for your own life.

What do you do that would cause people to be grateful for you?

_____

_____

_____

_____

A Sense of Purpose

Establishing goals and pursuing them with purpose is one of the key ways to reduce the amount of time you engage in unhealthy, unsafe, excessive sexual behaviors. This includes immersing yourself in a challenging experience and living in a state of flow, (performing an activity fully immersed in a feeling of energized focus, full involvement, and enjoyment in the process of the activity). Channeling mental attention into challenging activities can become most rewarding.

Identify some of the personal and professional goals
which might be able to provide you with a sense of purpose.
Write them or draw them below.

Personal Goals	Professional Goals

My Uplifting Thoughts ... or Not

We all have many different thoughts throughout the day. Some are helpful in overcoming an addiction to sex and some are not helpful.

List some of your thoughts that uplift you.

**List some of your thoughts that trigger an urge to
engage in excessive sexual behaviors.**

Core Beliefs

Many of the sex-based thoughts that run through your mind are a response to core beliefs you have about yourself and about intimate partners in your life. These rigid, core beliefs are related to how you view yourself, others, and experiences you have had in life.

Some of these beliefs might include one or more of the following:
- *"I will never find someone who understands me."* (personal)
- *"My partner offers little intimacy in our relationship."* (others)
- *"I always get rejected in social situations."* (life experience)

Now you add your own beliefs in the sections below.

How I View Myself

How I View Others

My Life Experiences

What I Need to Change

Am I in Denial?

Many people with an addiction to sex deny that they have a problem.

On the line under each example of sex-related denial, place an X on the continuum of how much you relate to the statement. On the dotted line below each one, write why you rated yourself that way. Be HONEST!

I don't believe I have a problem.

0 (Not Like Me)   5 (Somewhat Like Me)   10 (Much Like Me)

. . . .

I can quit any time I want to quit.

0 (Not Like Me)   5 (Somewhat Like Me)   10 (Much Like Me)

. . . .

Others are to blame for the way I behave.

0 (Not Like Me)   5 (Somewhat Like Me)   10 (Much Like Me)

. . . .

My sexual behaviors are not hurting my life.

0 (Not Like Me)   5 (Somewhat Like Me)   10 (Much Like Me)

. . . .

It's okay to think about sex as much as I do.

0 (Not Like Me)   5 (Somewhat Like Me)   10 (Much Like Me)

. . . .

I'm not the only one doing these types of things.

0 (Not Like Me)   5 (Somewhat Like Me)   10 (Much Like Me)

. . . .

I'm not hurting anyone.

0 (Not Like Me)   5 (Somewhat Like Me)   10 (Much Like Me)

. . . .

The Higher (Much Like Me) your score on each of the statements, the more you are denying your sexual addiction. Areas where you scored lower (Not Like Me) suggest that you are not in denial. Any scores other than 0 can be indicative of a sexual addiction problem.

© 2021 WHOLE PERSON ASSOCIATES, 101 WEST 2ND STREET, SUITE 203, DULUTH MN 55802 • 800-247-6789 • WHOLEPERSON.COM

The Life I Want

It is important to have a picture in mind of what you want your future life to look like. This visualization and working toward reaching it can help you think about your sexual behaviors and how those behaviors play into the picture.

In the box below, write a poem, letter, or essay about your life now.

In the box below, write a poem, letter, or essay about the life you want.

Draw Your Future

The use of drawing can help you express yourself and explore various aspects of a future which does not include excessive, unsafe, unhealthy sex. (Career, intimate relationships, family, friends, school, work, volunteer activities, etc.)

Draw your responses to the sentence starters below. Don't think too much about it, just start drawing! After you draw, describe what the picture means with one word or a short phrase.

A major goal I want to achieve...	I will be proud when ...
It means _____	It means _____
My future involves...	I am most productive when...
It means _____	It means _____

© 2021 WHOLE PERSON ASSOCIATES, 101 WEST 2ND STREET, SUITE 203, DULUTH MN 55802 • 800-247-6789 • WHOLEPERSON.COM

My Life Plan

All people, especially those addicted to sex, can benefit from a detailed life plan. Your life plan can encompass all of your hopes and dreams for your future. Start thinking about a plan to capture the life you want to start living today.

In the spaces that follow for the various areas of your life, create your goals and actions that you will take to reach these goals.

Areas of My Life	Short-Term Goal (Within 1-2 Years)	Long-Term Goal (5 years from now)	My Actions to Take to Reach My Goals
Family			
Career			
Health			
Financial Security			
Community Service			
Spirituality/ Religion			
Intimate Relationships			
Other			

Thought Tracking

After giving in to a sexual craving, it is helpful to gain insight by tracking the thoughts and emotions that were associated with the behavior. It's important to realize that when you are engaging in excessive unsafe, unhealthy sexual behaviors, you are taking time away from more productive, healthy behaviors and relationships.

Track some of these thoughts below:

My Thoughts & Emotions	Sexual Behavior	This Takes Me Away From
Example: I think about how bad my life is because I feel alone.	*I visit strip clubs a few times a week rather than spending time with family.*	*My connection with my family members. We are no longer close.*

Take accountability... blame is the water in which
many dreams and relationships drown.
~ **Steve Maraboli**

How does the above quotation apply to your life?

_____

_____

_____

I Am Proud ...

You are possibly ashamed of many of the sexual acts in which you have engaged over the years, but, hopefully you are proud of many things too, such as accomplishments, past situations, personal qualities, skills, and talents, and so much more.

Think about things you are proud of, and describe a dozen of them, in each of the boxes below. They can be big things like getting a new job or small things like working five days straight. When you are finished, cut them out and put them on sticky notes or tape them up in places where you will see them.

I am proud of

I am proud of

I am proud of

I am proud of

I am proud of

I am proud of

I am proud of

I am proud of

I am proud of

I am proud of

I am proud of

I am proud of

Great Goal-Setting - Steps 1 & 2

It is often difficult to become motivated and it is sometimes even more difficult to stay motivated, but setting goals with a plan can help.

To make sure your goals are clear and reachable, each goal should be SMART!
- Specific (simple, sensible, significant).
- Measurable (meaningful, motivating).
- Achievable (agreed, attainable).
- Relevant (reasonable, realistic and resourced, results-based).
- Time bound (time-based, time limited, time/cost limited, timely, time-sensitive).

Practice being S.M.A.R.T. with one of YOUR goals:

Write one of your generic personal or professional goals.

My goal is to _____

_____

_____

_____

_____

Step 1: Make your goal detailed and SPECIFIC.

Specifically, I will _____

_____

Step 2: Make your goal MEASUREABLE.

I will measure or track my goal by using these numbers or methods _____

_____

I will know I've reached my goal when_____

_____

_____

(Continued on the next page)

© 2021 WHOLE PERSON ASSOCIATES, 101 WEST 2ND STREET, SUITE 203, DULUTH MN 55802 • 800-247-6789 • WHOLEPERSON.COM

Great Goal-Setting - steps 3 & 4

Step 3: Make your goal ACHIEVEABLE.

Additional resources I need to achieve this goal:_____

_____

_____

Ways I will find the time: _____

_____

_____

Things I need to learn more about: _____

_____

People I can talk to for support: _____

_____

Step 4: Make your goal RELEVANT.

The reason I want to reach this goal is: _____

_____

_____

_____

_____

This goal is realistic because: _____

_____

_____

_____

Step 5: Make your goal TIME BOUND.

I will reach my main goal by (date) ____/____/____.

My halfway measurement will be _____ on (date) ____/____/____.

Additional dates and milestones I will aim for include _____

_____

_____

_____

What you get by achieving your goals is not as important as
what you become by achieving your goals.
~ Zig Ziglar

My Recovery Plan

The My Recovery Plan that follows will help you to deal with your sexual triggers. Use My Recovery Plan as a guide for making progress toward the cessation of your unhealthy sexual urges and triggers.

Complete the following steps for each action you will take.

Step 1: An action I will take to lessen my sexual cravings:

Step 2: One goal for my progress toward the completion of this action and a target date:

Step 3: Mini-actions I will take to attain the goal identified in Step 2:

Step 4: Are there any obstacles to the mini-actions from Step 3? How will I overcome the obstacles?

Step 5: The resources I both have and need to establish to overcome obstacles identified in Step 4:

Step 6: I will make these actions a habit by following these steps:

© 2021 WHOLE PERSON ASSOCIATES, 101 WEST 2ND STREET, SUITE 203, DULUTH MN 55802 • 800-247-6789 • WHOLEPERSON.COM

Rewarding Myself

It is important to remember to reward yourself when you avoid unhealthy sexual activities! This will motivate you to continue this behavior. The challenge is to decide what reward would motivate you to reach your goal. Your reward needs to be something that will give you the incentive to achieve your goal. It needs to be within your budget and something you'll be excited about.

Ex: I wanted to go to the strip club so badly, but instead I went to see my daughter sing a solo in a concert! It was great! I was so proud of her. She was very thrilled that I came!

Consider possible rewards for healthy behavior:
- A reward that would be meaningful to me._____
- A small reward I could give myself. _____
- A large reward I could give myself. _____
- A reward that would not cost money and would be fun. _____
- A reward I can afford and that would be fun. _____
- A reward I can enjoy alone._____
- A reward I can enjoy with the people who support me. _____

_____

_____

Rewards are designed to help you to pay attention to your triumphs, not your setbacks. Rewards will create good feelings and propel you to want to work harder to reach your goals. Whenever you have completed or achieved one of your goals, treat yourself to one of the items on your above list. You can also reward yourself by giving yourself positive affirmations when achieving a goal.

Guidelines for creating positive affirmations:

- Make the affirmations positive and realistic.
- Create affirmations that appeal to you and nobody else.
- Repeat them as often as possible.

Examples
I can enjoy a healthy, intimate relationship.
I will overcome my sexual addiction.
I am taking control of my life.
I am a happy and peaceful person.
I will make positive, healthy choices from now on.

Write your own affirmations in the boxes below and then transfer them onto sticky notes!

My Affirmations

Quotes about a Hopeful Future

On the lines that follow each of the four quotes, describe how the quote speaks to you and your future plans.

When it is obvious that the goals cannot be reached,
don't adjust the goals, adjust the action steps.
~ Confucius

_____

_____

_____

True happiness...is not attained through self-gratification,
but through fidelity to a worthy purpose.
~ Helen Keller

_____

_____

_____

It's exciting setting goals and moving forward with them.
~ Amber Frey

_____

_____

_____

The discipline you learn and character you build from setting and achieving a goal
can be more valuable than the achievement of the goal itself.
~ Bo Bennett

_____

_____

_____

Which quote especially speaks to you and your future goals and plans? Why?

_____

_____

_____

© 2021 WHOLE PERSON ASSOCIATES, 101 WEST 2ND STREET, SUITE 203, DULUTH MN 55802 • 800-247-6789 • WHOLEPERSON.COM

WholePerson

Whole Person Associates is the leading publisher of training resources for professionals who empower people to create and maintain healthy lifestyles. Our creative resources will help you work effectively with your clients in the areas of stress management, wellness promotion, mental health, and life skills.

Please visit us at our web site: **WholePerson.com**. You can check out our entire line of products, place an order, request our print catalog, and sign up for our monthly special notifications.

Whole Person Associates
800-247-6789
Books@WholePerson.com